Fasting

WHAT · WHY · HOW

Niklaus Brantschen

CROSSROAD PUBLISHING COMPANY

NEW YORK

Original publication: *Fasten neu erleben: Warum, wie, wozu?* By Herder Verlag, Freiburg, Basle, and Vienna 2006.

First published in the English language in 2010 in the United States by The Crossroad Publishing Company www.CrossroadPublishing.com

English translation © 2010 by The Crossroad Publishing Company

All rights reserved. No part of this book may be reproduced, stored in a retrieval system, or transmitted, in any form or by any means, electronic, mechanical, photocopying, recording, or otherwise, without the written permission of The Crossroad Publishing Company.

In continuation of our 200-year tradition of independent publishing, The Crossroad Publishing Company proudly offers a variety of books with strong, original voices and diverse perspectives. The viewpoints expressed in our books are not necessarily those of The Crossroad Publishing Company, any of its imprints or of its employees. No claims are made or responsibility assumed for any health or other benefit.

Book produced by Scribe Inc. (http://www.scribenet.com)

Printed in the United States of America

Library of Congress Cataloging-in-Publication Data is available from the Library of Congress.

ISBN-13: 978-0-8245-2540-8 (cloth)

ISBN-10: 0-8245-2540-X (cloth)

1 2 3 4 5 6 7 8 9 10 15 14 13 12 11 10

Contents

To the Reader

Fasting is much discussed and written about these days. More and more people wish to experience its effects themselves, but at the same time, they fear it. This is because they find fasting to be simultaneously fascinating and alarming: it attracts and repels; it seems to make sense and yet is hard to comprehend. Fasting is a process that appears easy to endure but is still an adventure waiting to be risked. Maybe you have asked yourself, should I do it or not? And, in the end, you have found reasons to defer this beneficial.

With this little book I want to introduce you to the ways of fasting or, if you have fasted at some earlier time, to remind you of its benefits. My main goal, therefore, is to strengthen your confidence in your ability to fast and to encourage you to try fasting when the time is ripe.

—Niklaus Brantschen

Introduction

What Is Fasting?

People are developing a deeper understanding of fasting, a practice steeped in tradition and spread across all cultures and religions. But they also have misunderstandings about it. These misunderstandings usually arise where only *one* aspect of fasting is taken into consideration: for instance, only the health aspect, or just the spiritual or sociopolitical one. We also encounter notions of fasting related to weight-loss diets, mandatory religious fasting, or a certain kind of hunger strike. In addition to these "major" misconceptions, which I expand on in appendix 1, there are some minor, less misleading misunderstandings that have more to do with linguistic usage than with the practice itself. However, these aspects can help clarify the meaning and advantages of fasting. I mention four such errors.

When We Sleep We Do Not Fast

We occasionally hear people say that fasting is an everyday or, even better, an every night thing. That is, because normally we do not eat at night, we therefore "fast." The word breakfast sheds light on this concept as it refers to "breaking the fast." The French take their time with this: they break the nightly "fasting" (*jeune*) only at lunchtime (*déjeuner*) and only break the fast with something small in the morning (*petit déjeuner*).

However, taking these words in their literal sense confuses the matter. The point is, when we sleep we do not fast. Rather, fasting is done when one is conscious. The passive process of not eating when asleep does not suffice. A wakeful, inner readiness is essential for fasting, for doing without food for a shorter or longer period of time.

When We Are Sick We Do Not Fast

The idea that we fast when we are sick is erroneous, as well. When we lose our appetite and are therefore unable to consume anything, that does not count as fasting; it is simply loss of appetite.

Animals Do Not Fast

The same applies when human fasting is compared with the eating habits of animals. Many think that animals in the wild fast for weeks and months—as a part of their normal annual rhythm. The end of winter and feeding on fresh greens in the sunny edges of the forest is a great experience for the animals. But this is only fasting in its figurative sense. Strictly speaking, animals do not fast. Fasting is something human. It refers to a dimension where freedom and decision making play an important role.

Starving Is Not Fasting

Another common misunderstanding is mistaking starvation for fasting. The linguistic usage was ambiguous for a long time, as ancient fasting literature talks of "starvation diets." Today, however, we always associate starvation with poverty, fear, and despair. But fasting is about optimism and the joy of practicing something healing in spite of the challenges. In other words, when starving, we do not fast. But, as we will see, the reverse also holds true: when we fast, we do not starve.

Fasting is thus more than not eating. But what does it really mean? We can attempt a short, provisional description of fasting based on the factors we have addressed so far.

In brief, fasting is

- a wakeful (we do not fast in our sleep),
- active (as opposed to passive noneating such as during sickness),

- human occurrence (animals do not fast),
- in which body and soul are able to draw nourishment not from the outside but from the inside, from one's own deposits,
- for a certain period of time,
- without disdain for food.

In this process, a pleasant feeling of lightness, particularly in movement and breathing, sets in, along with deep relaxation and peace, after minor initial complaints like nervousness, headache, and pangs of appetite.

Fasting is something comprehensive and complete and can be seen both subjectively and objectively:

- *Subjective*: Fasting challenges the whole person—body, mind, and spirit—including all of our willing capacity.
- *Objective*: One-sided descriptions do not do justice to fasting. It is just like in the story of the blind men trying to describe an elephant.

According to an ancient Persian story, a king and his army came in the vicinity of a city whose citizens were blind. The king owned a powerful elephant that was trained to be used in attacks. The people of the city were eager to acquaint themselves with the elephant. Some set out and went to the elephant and touched it, blindly. When they returned to their fellow citizens, they were asked about the elephant's build and structure. The man who had felt the elephant's ear said, "It is a huge, rough being, broad and wide like a blanket." And the one who had touched the trunk said, "I know what it is really like. It is like a straight and hollow pipe, frightening and dangerous!" But the person who had touched the elephant's foot and legs said, "He is powerful and almost like a pillar."

Each one understood something; but no one understood it wholly. And even the parts—the ear, trunk, legs—together, did not form the elephant, since the whole is more than its parts put together. What is needed is an overall view. The same applies to fasting, where material and spiritual, natural and supernatural, individual and social factors fuse together in an inseparable way.

© Bhupi - Fotolia.com

Part I

Fasting: What For and Why?

Lo behold the effects of fasting!
It heals diseases
chases away blasphemous thoughts,
gives the spirit greater clarity
and leads man to the throne of God.

—St. Athanasius, *De Virginitate* (295–373)

The various effects of fasting have been known since time immemorial. They help to transform one's relationship with oneself, with God, and with other human beings. In other words, they are part of the mind-body-soul, spiritual, and social realms. Here, it may be repeated that all three realms are closely related to each other and form a whole. We would thus rather talk of them as *dimensions* rather than as realms.

To begin, let us focus on all those aspects of fasting that relate to observation and experience—that is, the body-soul and health elements. Fasting is certainly not only a physical and psychic process, but we do well not to neglect these dimensions of the practice.

1

Health

Doctors discovered the benefits of fasting in the nineteenth century, but the history of this new, medicinal fasting has not been widely documented. But the names of those who rediscovered fasting, often independent of each other and in different parts of the world, deserve our attention:

- Two Americans: Dr. Heinz Fahrner underwent a fourteen-day fasting regimen in the summer of 1880 that was much publicized by the American and European presses; and Dr. Edward Hooker Dewey went through three-, four-, and five-week fasting regimens and became the talk of the town across America.
- Dr. von Seeland, a Russian, was convinced as early as 1887,[1] as a result of his experiments and personal experiences, that fasting is not just therapeutic, but rather has more of a hygienic and pedagogic significance.

- Dr. Guillaume Guelpa, a Frenchman, produced books and methodology—*la méthode Guelpa*—that became famous all over Europe.[2]
- Dr. Gustav Riedlin of Freiburg was doyen of the German doctors who propagated fasting—whom we can thank for many popular scientific works.
- Friedrich von Segesser, a Swiss doctor, wrote a scientific text on fasting that was praised by the therapeutic fasting pioneer Otto Buchinger as a "thorough and insightful book."
- Two further books also deserve mention: Otto Buchinger's classic *Das Heilfasten: Und seine Hilfsmethoden* (*The Therapeutic Fasting Cure*), and Heinz Fahrner's standard work *Fasten als Therapie* (*Fasting as Therapy*).

Thanks to the new medicinal science—particularly that of Otto Buchinger and Heinz Fahrner—we are in a position to explain the curative effects of fasting and gain insight into the physical and spiritual effects of this experience.

A Process of Transformation

Fasting is occasionally compared to the eating patterns of several animals. This comparison, though imperfect, is somewhat correct. Just like animals, human beings have retained the ability, gained thousands of years ago, of shifting from external to internal nourishment, of mobilizing and processing proteins and fat reserves deposited in the body and thereby providing it with nutrition from its well-stocked reserve. This ability of entire clans and masses to survive in winter or during famines has become stunted today, but fasting can revive it.

The transformation to fasting is not automatic; it is not like a radio that you can switch from the electrical network, the external power supply, to a battery, the internal power supply, with the push of a button. Rather, it is a holistic, psychophysical process that can be simplified or complicated depending on the extent of one's inner willingness to get involved in and adapt oneself to the process. Biologically, the process of fasting is as follows.

It begins with bowel evacuation. The best way to do this is by using Epsom salt or through enemas. As a result, the bowel movements, the so-called peristalsis, come to a stop, the bowel volume decreases considerably, and the digestive secretions, including saliva, diminish. There is sticky saliva in the mouth. Headache and dizziness may be observed. Moreover, it is not uncommon for those who are fasting to be overcome by a strange, agitated nervousness. But once the body and the soul become accustomed to not having external intake, the feeling of hunger and the sticky saliva are also held at bay. The immobilization of the digestive organs gives rise to a pleasant feeling of lightness, especially when moving or breathing. The headaches disappear. The initial nervousness and the aggressive restlessness give way to relaxation and peace.

There are reasons for all this, which I would like to touch upon briefly, as my personal experience has taught me that getting an insight into the fasting regimen is of great help in enduring its initial discomforts. Headache and dizziness, among other things, are caused by an initial drop in blood pressure. Nervousness can be attributed to the fear of not being used to fasting, the secret worry of being unable to live without food or not surviving through an extreme situation. This fear leads to a high adrenaline rush and thus to the common side effects that the mere thought of fasting can trigger. These symptoms often arise as soon as the course of fasting begins. Although the fear one has about the extreme situation at the beginning of a course of fasting is actually justified, once a person overcomes this fear physically and, more importantly, psychologically, one's adrenaline level falls below the normal limit. This in turn explains the feeling of relaxation and peace after the change.

The Unhealthy Disappears, the Healthy Persists

By switching from external to internal nourishment, what primarily happens during fasting is that structures and substances that disturb the cell state are destroyed and broken down. As a rule of thumb, 50 percent of an organism's cells are completely functional, 25 percent are newly formed, and 25 percent are aging, unhealthy, or dying. Fasting applies to this last 25 percent. "The unhealthy disappears, the healthy persists," says Otto Buchinger concisely, and Heinz Fahrner attributes the "profound self-cleansing in all organs" to the body's switchover to internal nutrition and digestion.

Incidentally, this general cleansing is often associated with certain problems, which particularly make their presence felt on critical days. These days should not be confused with the critical days at the beginning of the fasting period; they normally crop up every seven days. It is astounding that the organism is in harmony with the biblical seven-day rhythm in its task of purifying and cleansing the body.

But how does one explain these problems? Why do scars from operations and accidents suddenly start hurting on a critical day? Fahrner explains this using the example of a fifty-year-old fasting patient. One night, this patient woke up with a piercing pain in his right eye. Nothing that could explain the pain could be seen outwardly. The patient remembered having suffered a stab injury on the outside of his right eye when he was young. The fine scar from this wound was then "treated" through fasting and removed. Consequently, the pain disappeared and the eye healed.

What applies to invisible injuries and scars also holds true for chronic diseases of the connective tissues, which are also aptly called storage tissues. These diseases can resurface and can be cured by fasting. This explains the acute rheumatism attacks in rheumatic patients or migraine attacks in migraine patients at the onset of fasting. Those who fast relive their illness but only briefly, ultimately to cure it in due course. As Heinz Fahrner wrote in his standard work on fasting,

> Since fasting has an effect on the entire cell system right up to the molecular structure, all individual medical history related changes, problems, deposits, and immunizations in the relevant organs, cell structures and basic elements of connective tissues are addressed.
>
> The most recent changes are the easiest and the quickest to be treated; the oldest ones are the most tedious and difficult. We can only reach the older layers of our physical past with prolongation of fasting. The distinctly changeable fasting process in fact demonstrates the once healthy and harmonious life stages on the one hand and the unhealthy, diseased ones on the other: fasting recapitulates one's own medical history.[3]

© Elenathewise - Fotolia.com

Fahrner's text illustrates the basic principle of healing through fasting, making evident why fasting has proven itself to be "an operation without a knife" in almost all frequently occurring illnesses. All acute and chronic inflammations call for a cleansing fast. Indeed, many doctors who employ fasting as a natural healing process have told me that obesity has attracted their attention recently through a roundabout way of other illnesses that can be treated by fasting.

Prevention Is Better than Cure

As we all know, prevention is better than cure. Otto Buchinger clearly emphasized this with regard to fasting. For him, preventive fasting was the ultimate goal of medical endeavors. Fasting by so-called healthy persons for reasons of awareness, fitness, blood purification, and inner tuning, rather than to increase longevity, is more important than fasting by ill persons.[4]

Buchinger himself went down the path from curative to preventive fasting, and he traced the steps of this course. He described himself as "completely suffering" from chronic rheumatism with muscular atrophy, hepatomegaly (enlarged liver), and a recurring gall bladder inflammation and began fasting on the advice of a friend. A nineteen-day fasting treatment with the famous fasting doctor Gustav Riedlin in Freiburg freed him of rheumatism, and a subsequent four-week strict fasting treatment even cured him of his persistent liver and gall bladder problems.

This second round of fasting had an additional element that Buchinger called "discovery of one's self." Later he wondered why he did not experience this additional element during the first round and came up with the explanation that, on the one hand, he was not spiritually open for the more profound effects of fasting and, on the other hand, a large part of his energy was consumed by the life-saving recovery process. This important discovery helped Buchinger to highlight the decisive role of motivation while fasting and to advocate that even, and mainly, healthy persons should fast.

Fasting cures and prevents illnesses by eliminating them biologically. That is only a part of how this happens, however. Equally important is a practically formulated fasting period, which helps one keep a check on eating and other daily habits and to change them if required, thereby leading to a healthier and better life.

And since body and soul are one, and what is good for the body is also good for the soul, the mental and spiritual effects of fasting cannot be overlooked.

2

Spirituality

It is a common misconception that the more radical the fasting, the greater and better its effects. Indeed, it is wise to be prepared, it is helpful to follow a proven method, and the ease acquired through continual practice is desirable. But fasting should never become a feat of bravery. Otherwise, it no longer will work as medicine but will become a poison. If taken as a record-breaking performance—that is, the more, the better—it only pampers the ego instead of putting it into perspective and assigning it its rightful place.

Thus, fasting is exposed to the perils of pride. I do not mean the rightful pride and joy that we experience when overcoming the fear of the unknown and taking the risk of fasting. I mean, rather, condescending behavior toward others who have not yet comprehended fasting and are still caught up in the dregs of worldly needs. The Bible warns against the display of fasting just like the display of praying and giving alms (Matthew 6). The deeper cause of arrogance is inherent in the process of fasting itself.

After finding ourselves somewhat down and in a depressed mood during the early days of a fast, we can become quite elated. We may feel light and buoyant, which can put us in danger of overestimating our abilities and becoming reckless. Only when we overcome this temptation of pride can the spiritual fruits of fasting ripen: self-awareness, self-discovery, and the experience of God.

Fasting and Finding Yourself

How can I find myself? How do I know myself? Who am I? These questions have existed for as long as humans have lived on this earth, and they are vital questions. The command of the Oracle of Delphi, "Know thyself," was considered sacred and was engraved on a temple. Only in recent times has the endeavor to discover and find oneself fallen into disrepute. On the one hand, we have become strangers to ourselves and to others and, like the psychoanalyst Erich Fromm, we might experience ourselves as "human fragments." On the other hand, this need has brought forth numerous, often unqualified, proposals, which with great marketing savvy promise help and in turn have triggered a self-discovery boom. Yet these often do not cure their followers and only leave them in the lurch. The vicious circle is perfect. Now, how does one come out of it? Lamenting is of little help. And worse, some indiscriminately condemn the deep-rooted human pursuit for self-discovery along with its exploitation and simplification through certain psycho-, socio-, astro-, or other "ologies" that claim to be based on science.

On the contrary, what is called for is thoughtful analysis, which takes into account the depth and breadth of true self-knowledge and self-discovery. Therefore, the question arises: Is fasting, if understood correctly, an effective way to self-discovery? And if so, then why?

As explained earlier, during fasting the human body shifts from external to internal nourishment. The result of this psychosomatic process is that we go from "being outside of ourselves" to becoming the "center of our being," where we can enter a state of rest and relaxation. In other words, this change of direction or "switchover" facilitates meditation and self-discovery. During fasting sessions, I often experience that my fellow participants intuitively seek silence and calm. Fasting leads to calmness and induces meditation; meditation, in turn, favors and intensifies the fasting experience. Both together help us understand ourselves better. Why?

Let us assume that we are disappointed with a person dear to us, stressed because of some unpleasant work, or frustrated because it has rained on a holiday. In such situations, we might say, "I am not feeling well. I need something." This "something" could refer to an understanding person, an enjoyable activity, or even a walk outside for fresh air. Instead, we might think of this "something" as "something *to eat*." This substitute activity results because the feeling of emptiness and frustration is like a twin to the feeling of hunger. The drive to eat is the most fundamental of all drives and is insatiable. Language expresses this, for example, when we talk of hungering and thirsting after love, justice, or peace.

When we cannot satisfy this hunger adequately, we become prone to compensatory acts and substitutes such as medications, drugs, alcohol, or, in fact, food, empty activity, and idle gossip. Eating, just like talking, is a tried-and-tested means to suppress and forget unpleasant aspects and to prevent deep-seated feelings of discomfort from surfacing. And herein lies the opportunity fasting provides, when combined with periods of silence and meditative practices. When fasting, we give up surrogate satisfactions that so often manipulate and blind us. As Benedictine monk Anselm Grün wrote, "Fasting reveals to me who I am."[1]

This insight matches with Mahatma Gandhi's experience: when he undertook a fast in November 1925, as repentance on somebody's behalf for an offense in the Sabarmati Ashram, he confessed that fasting was a part of his being. For Gandhi, doing without fasting was like doing without his eyes. Fasting did for the inner world what eyes did for the outer.

Fasting means a better discovery of one's self and one's path; it also means experiencing ourselves as limited, dependent, and yet as free. This seeming contradiction needs a short explanation: when fasting, our bodies sustain themselves from our own reserves, thus we literally live off ourselves. This has a brightening effect on our mood, yet it also is at the bottom of our feelings of freedom and sovereignty. But we also experience, in just as existential a way, that we are dependent on other human beings, on water and air, on plants and animals, and that we can neither exist out of ourselves nor do we want to.

This experience can make us deeply grateful. Thus, during fasting, we become aware of how close arrogance, humility, and self-knowledge reside within us.

Fasting and the Experience of God

"The evidence from all times and all zones confirms that fasting elicits spiritual powers, supernatural 'magical' powers and conditions that foster contact with the transcendental world."[2] When I first read this sentence by Dr. Claude Régamey, I was taken aback. I wondered why the author had put the word *magical* in quotation marks. Then, I understood its significance from the context: here, Régamey points to a danger that we have already come across, that of arrogance: the danger of turning fasting into a magic formula, in order to usurp God's power and to acquire it in a material way. Does it have to be this way? Is there any good, light magic in addition to evil magic—some clever and perhaps forgotten powers that humans have, which are activated through fasting? My opinion is yes; here is why.

The physiological switchover to the inside that comes along with fasting—the "walking toward one-self," the "being with oneself," and the strange state of mind during night hours, which people who are fasting spend in contemplative wakefulness or asleep in deep guiding dreams—can activate our receptivity for transcendence, can let us hear what otherwise we might not listen to, and can let us see what otherwise we might overlook.

In the words of the German mystic and poet Angelus Silesius,

> He who has taken
> his senses within
> hears what is unsaid
> and sees in the night

Some references from the Bible and tradition, as well as from many other sources, substantiate this sensitivity and vision fostered by fasting. After three weeks of fasting, the prophet Daniel experienced a revelation that is specified as the result of his fast that he undertook for the sake of others (Daniel 10). We know of Moses and Elijah, the two leading represen-tatives of the law and of prophecy, who, during their respective forty-day fasts on Mt. Horeb, were given an overwhelming experience of God (Deuteronomy 9; 1 Kings 19).

The desert fathers, knowing that overeating deadens the "sharp vision of the heart" (Cassian), never tired of propagating fasting, in the interest of better clarity and insight. In the fifth century, Philoxenes, bishop in Syria, claimed that a person free from the "veil of a fatty heart" begins to discover that "more exists than what we see and grasp."

Indeed, there is something more than what we can see with our eyes and hold with our hands. In what follows I want to present a few key concepts to help explain how fasting helps us to experience that reality in addition to or, better, *within* the tangible and visible world, which we tend to call "God."

Fasting and Hope

One need not be pessimistic to say that hopelessness is widespread. Many of those who possess everything expect nothing more from the future or at least nothing good. Our Western world appears to be tired and old. Resignation is on the rise.

In this situation, fasting takes on an important role. Fasting, combined with prayers and meditation, has a lot to do with hope. The story is told of a former prisoner of war who was able to transform forced hunger into a fasting of his own free will. "I believe," he said, "that we must emphasize the deep

and fundamental link between fasting and hope. . . .
Fasting means to resist the 'ways of this world' and
give preference to 'being' over 'doing,' contemplation
over production, and the supernatural 'You will have'
over the natural 'Here you have it.'"

As human beings we exist in this tension of "have"
and "will have," of "already" and "not yet." We try
to circumvent this tension by choosing earthly life:
"eating and drinking like there is no tomorrow." Or
we dissipate this tension by opting exclusively for the
hereafter; then we strive to escape the demands of the

© Vitaliy Pakhnyushchyy - Fotolia.com

world and of people. But we can also bear this tension; moreover, we can transform it into something fruitful and productive. Hope strengthened by fasting allows us a glimpse of the "new creation" for which all creatures yearn, and its order of freedom and harmony from the "not yet" into our "already."

This "other" world has been referred to as the *kingdom of God*. It is not a world that can be found beyond or near or behind this world, and it is also not one that we will have access to in the future. Rather, it is a world that we are a part of here and at this moment. We do not come to the kingdom of God at the end of the world, after the horizontal expanse of this time and history until the end of times. This kingdom of God is already here; it is within us, and fasting can open our eyes to it.

Fasting and Prayer

Isaac of Nineveh summarizes the spiritual fasting experiences of the Eastern Orthodox Church hermits and monks by saying, "Indeed, once we begin to fast the spirit moves us to begin a conversation with God. The body that fasts cannot endure passing through the night on its bedstead alone, but fasting naturally urges to wake in God's company, not only in the day but also at night. The body of a person who fasts does not have a hard time battling sleep."[3] These words draw an understanding nod from all those who have fasted at least once. How can this literal wakefulness at night and the strange, responsive, open state of mind, incited to pray in the day, be explained?

Switching over to inner nourishment saves quite some energy and makes you feel rested and fresh when getting up even with less. Moreover, fasting reduces the amount of adrenaline in the body, which has a relaxing effect. On the other hand, noradrenalin levels rise, which has a stimulating effect and fosters active dreaming during sleep.

Good fasting doctors recommend spending the wakeful, high-spirited hours of the night in particular in contemplative reading and reflection. This is because "often, suppressed insights or completely new ideas surface, and bring solutions to problems that one may have sought for unsuccessfully for long time."[4]

The decisive question is, can I use this rare opportunity, become the subject, and creatively shape *even* the nightly fasting "event," or do I continue to be in the role of the object, merely suffering from sleeplessness? Then we may have beautiful experiences, for example, a childhood or other prayer, dear but "forgotten," suddenly resurfaces and stays with us. We can say then, *It* prays from within me.

We also need to mention fasting dreams in this context. They often have such a lasting impact that there is hardly anything that can be done in the morning but to write them down. Dreams during fasting pass through all levels of our soul space and are clear and lucid. It is worthwhile to ponder the extent to which the great prophetic dreams in the Bible and other holy scriptures have actually been dreams during fasting.

Fasting and Celebration

We tend to associate fasting with images of harsh days and gloomy faces; and feasting with the sound of laughter and the clink of glasses. The contrast between fast and feast seems absolute. However, appearances can be deceptive. "The matter is more complicated, and yet simpler. Spiritual sacrifice aims to leave behind the contrast between suffering and joy in a kind of 'alchemy of pain,' in which suffering is alike the inward face of highest joy."[5]

Fasting is closely related to death. Eating means to live; not eating in the long run means to die. And just as death is a preparation for a new birth, a resurrection, so is fasting. Thus, there is some deeper logic in the church's talk of "celebrating the period of fasting." Fasting finds an analogy during festivals, especially during Easter, but not just in its chronological succession and not even in the sense of better enjoyment of festive food after deprivation. There is a much deeper association: it pertains to death and the joy of a renewed sense of being. The bishop, Basil the Great (about 330–79), who was trained in the desert, also appeals not to put down the days of fasting but to live them in a state of happiness: "Do not be distressed when you are being healed. Foolish is the one who does not rejoice because of the health of the soul."[6]

This joy cannot be understood by itself. It is rather a question of deeper motivation. The prayer that encourages fasting and elevates the heart is of great significance. The liturgy of Lent invites us to pray for this joy: "We beg you God Almighty that through the discipline of solemn fasting, this holy penance, we also find joy."

Fast becomes feast. Surely, we are not to choose and mix as we please. As the sixteenth-century mystic Teresa of Avila said so well, "When you fast, you fast; when you eat partridge, you eat partridge." And it is true: this does not exclude but includes the fact that in voluntary, self-directed abstinence, there lies great joy and freedom. We have seen that fasting—when undefeated by the danger of arrogance—fosters self-discovery and self-knowledge, on the one hand, and the opening and a strange awareness of the transcendent, on the other, thanks to the "switchover to the inside." But spiritually organized fasting only becomes an actual *healing fast* when it takes the laws of body and soul and the medical and psychological findings seriously.

What Is *Curative* Fasting?

Fasting draws its powers from the integration of natural, psychosomatic, and medically verifiable facts as well as from a deeper, holistic, and finally spiritual motivation. Both dimensions—and incidentally, even the social dimension—combine and are mutually conditional. If we decide to apply the question of what came first, the chicken or the egg, to medically and religiously motivated fasting, the answer would be that fasting is as original as religion.

Fasting has benefitted religion just as religion has promoted fasting and, through wise rules, prevented abuse.

In recent times, Otto Buchinger—for whom "praying and fasting" belonged together like "inhaling and exhaling," like "above and below," like "heaven and earth"—coined a wide-ranging, all-encompassing term for fasting motivated by health concerns and religious inspiration. He called it the "curative fasting." The root word *curative* includes the following aspects:

- Medical curing (*curare*)
- Psychosomatic curing and becoming whole (*integritas*)
- Salvation promised by God (*salus*)
- Finding the holy within this world (*sanctum*)[7]

What is missing in this definition of the term "healing fast" are the social and political dimensions (or the combined sociopolitical dimension). The sociopolitical dimension does not surface in Buchinger's book at all, apart from the mention of "peoples' well-being" and "peoples' health." In spite of this criticism, it is Buchinger's most lasting merit that he has recombined at least two aspects of fasting: fasting as therapy and spiritually motivated fasting.

One can hope that, in fasting, the new medical findings and the ancient religious, Christian, and non-Christian insights continue to be combined into a comprehensive motivation. This happens where the demands of Otto Buchinger are met: "The object is not the [medical] technology, but what fasting sanctifies. The doctor, who speaks of curative fasting, should not lack pastoral experience and the pastor should not be entirely lacking in medical experience."[8]

The relationship between purely medical and religiously motivated fasting can be explained using an illustration of a princess and a prince where the princess, who has been asleep for a long time under a spell (religious fasting), is awakened by the proud prince of modern medicine (medical fasting). The two make a good pair—the princess brings inexhaustible riches into the marriage as a dowry—and even the prince is not empty-handed, thanks to the "knowledge" that he has. Moreover, both discover themselves again, and in earlier times, both the religious and the medical were one, as priests were still doctors and doctors were also priests.

Does that sound a little too fairytale-like? Is it presumptuous to hope that the old family feud between science and religion can finally be resolved even in this point, in favor of this fortunate pair? Together, the prince and princess—the clinical, somewhat sterile and well-informed fasting combined with that which is traditional, religious, and passive—form a powerful and effective holy whole, which benefits the body and soul, as well as other humans and the world, as we will soon see.

3

Sociopolitical Aspects

From a superficial point of view, it might appear that the physiological process of fasting results in withdrawal—making a person egoistic, unsocial, and apolitical. That is a danger, of which prophets and, later, the desert fathers and teachers of the church never grew weary of warning. We have a relevant text in the book of the prophet Isaiah:

> Behold, ye fast for strife and debate, and to smite with the fist of wickedness:
>> ye shall not fast as ye do this day, to make your voice to be heard on high.
>
> Is it such a fast that I have chosen? a day for a man to afflict his soul?
>> is it to bow down his head as a bulrush, and to spread sackcloth and ashes under him?
>> wilt thou call this a fast, and an acceptable day to the LORD?

> Is not this the fast that I have chosen? to loose
> the bands of wickedness, to undo the heavy bur-
> dens, and to let the oppressed go free, and that
> ye break every yoke?
> Is it not to deal thy bread to the hungry, and
> that thou bring the poor that are cast out to thy
> house?
>> when thou seest the naked, that thou cover
>> him; and that thou hide not thyself from
>> thine own flesh? . . .
> If thou take away from the midst of thee the
> yoke, the putting forth of the finger, and speak-
> ing vanity;
> And if thou draw out thy soul to the hungry, and
> satisfy the afflicted soul;
>> then shall thy light rise in obscurity, and thy
>> darkness be as the noonday.
>
> (Isaiah 58:4–7, 9b–10)

These prophetic words do not leave any room for doubt: fasting means serving fellow humans. Where this does not hold true, it becomes perverted and loses its meaning.

Fasting and Sharing

Fasting is not an individual discipline; it is also not a combination of two things, namely fasting and spiritu-ality. It is essentially a combination of three factors: fast-ing, spirituality, and solidarity. The deuterocanonical

Old Testament text of Tobit mentions "fasting, praying, giving alms" (Tobit 12:8).

"Giving alms"—today, this term often sounds almost harmless. However, its intention is not so harmless, certainly not in the ancient texts. Consider what the philosopher Aristides said in his *Apology* addressed to Emperor Hadrian in the year 128 CE: "And if there is among them any that is poor and needy, and if they have no spare food, they fast two or three days in order to supply to the needy their lack of food."[1] Similarly, it is said in the book *The Shepherd of Hermas* (5.3) from the year 150: "You should only consume water and bread on the day of your fast. Then, you should give the amount that you would have spent on nourishment to a widow, an orphan or somebody needy. In this way, you should deprive yourself of something, so that someone else can derive benefits from your abstinence." Even in the ancient *Didascalia* scriptures (XIX, 1), fasting has been explained with regard to the plight of others—"But if there be a man who has nothing, let him fast, and that which would have been spent by him that day let him give for his brethren."[2]

Fasting means serving fellow humans. Admittedly, and this is often overlooked, it does not mean only distributing what is saved. It involves much more. Those who not only make do with just soup but who fast in a comprehensive sense over a period of time feel oneness with others and become more sensitive to their physical and mental plight. Twentieth-century Italian philosopher Lanza del Vasto expresses this experience in the following words: "He who fasts becomes transparent. The others become transparent to him. He feels their pains and he is defenseless against this. Thus, a human, who does not wish to be consumed by charity, should clog up all his senses through good food."[3]

As far as the vulnerability and the pain caused by fasting are concerned, I experienced a classic example of a common misunderstanding during a panel discussion on television several years ago: The host quoted the above-mentioned sentence by del Vasto. A participant in the discussion promptly replied, "In such a case, the fasting doctor must help and administer a homeopathic painkiller." What disregard for the deeper meaning concealed in fasting! As if we could love without it ever hurting.

When we fast the right way, we couldn't be further from becoming egotistical. On the contrary, fasting fosters compassion as sharing feels increasingly natural, and one feels a deep need to explain connectedness with others. But fasting affects not only our individual relationships; it is meaningful especially amid the current course of the whole world.

Fasting for Justice and Peace

Fasting leads to a deep bond with ourselves, with our fellow human beings, and with nature, which gives us air to breathe and water to drink, which nourishes us and from which we live. The effect of this deep bonding is an increasing willingness to do the utmost that one can, for justice, peace, and the conservation of creation.

Many people already practice "sustainable" eating habits based in a "conscientious world awareness," giving fasting regular presence in their lives. Such diets are characterized by an active consideration for those who suffer from hunger as well as toward future generations.

A good example for this comes from the diary of a student who took part in a group I had organized fasting for justice, peace, and the conservation of creation. I had asked the participants to record their insights and experiences, and one student wrote,

> Today, life for most people in our part of the world is dictated by the possibilities offered by an industrial civilization: more, better, prettier, faster. The practice of this ideology has resulted in the unfair distribution of available goods, the buildup of weapons for the sake of protecting this "excess," and the exploitation or destruction of the environment. We will not be able to combat these man-made dangers to our world unless we radically shift our thinking with regard to our understanding of the quality of life. We must come out of the "more and more" logic, one of constant increase; only then will it be possible for all those living now and those who will live in the future to survive on this planet.

For me, fasting means to practice this shift in my thinking. To a small extent, it means moving away from the mechanisms of daily life and reflecting. For a short while, I will live a life contradictory to my daily routine.

When we abstain from food together with others, we find our lives enriched in a way very different from the norms of success and consumerism, as we experience that less can be more. By learning with our entire being, with body and mind, that it is possible to make do with very little, we become aware that we do not need everything. At the same time, we realize what we need to live and what most people do not have in abundance.

The temporary abstinence from food encourages us to be careful with the gifts of creation. We learn to newly perceive food as a gift—a gift that we may use but not abuse. These gifts are available on this earth in abundance, and all people have equal rights to them. In this context, fasting for me means taking a step toward practicing the kind of self-constraint, which transforms today's dire need and is called for ethically.

When we fast, we feel ourselves and the world around us as never before. And this, for me, is the most exciting discovery from fasting: that I become fully alive, wholly compassionate toward myself, others, and the world that surrounds me. Engagement with justice, peace, and the conservation of creation is not possible without our endurance.

For me, this reflection is a sign of encouragement. When, sensitized through the fasting experience, we begin to love life so much that we are willing to engage fully in the work for a more just world, resignation gives way to a preparedness for change.

During a fast at the time of the first Gulf War, I experienced how those who fasted rapidly came out of their roles as spectators, and declared their solidarity with the innumerable victims not shown by the media, in silence and hours of prayer. At the same time, they asked themselves, what can I do to establish peace here, where I am?

Fasting is related to peace. There are more than enough examples to prove this. For example, I recall the story of Brother Nicholas of Flüe,[4] whose emblematic ways of life were a stark contrast to the eating and

© Helder Almeida - Fotolia.com

drinking sprees of his time. It is no coincidence that he became an instrument of peace and reconciliation from the calm and seclusion of the Ranft, thanks to his prayers and radical fasting. For the Swiss, he is the rescuer of their nation; on December 22, 1481, his advice prevented a civil war and made the Treaty of Stans possible, which served as the legal foundation for the Swiss Confederation for more than three hundred years. "Politics from silence, supported by fasting"— this is how the historical significance of the hermits from the Ranft can be described.

Or consider Gandhi's fasting campaigns in the service of peace and freedom. He advocated fasting as a nonviolent method in the fight for justice. "If the war that we are trying to prevent with all our might should take place and if it remains nonviolent as it should, with regard to its success, then fasting must play an important role."[5] Today, Gandhi is held up as a model by various fasting campaigns aiming to promote justice and peace.

Linking back once more to the early Christian tradition, let us turn again to Saint Basil the Great:

If only everyone who needs a counselor would take her in, there would be nothing preventing a deep peace from abiding in each house. Nations wouldn't be attacking each other, and armies wouldn't be engaging in battle. Neither would weapons be forged, if fasting ruled. There would be no point in holding court, prisons would be unpopulated, and evildoers wouldn't have a place to hide. If slanderers were found in the cities, they would be thrown into the sea.

It's clear that fasting would not only teach self-control in relation to all kinds of foods, but also how to entirely escape and get rid of covetousness, greed, and all kinds of evil. Having been set free, nothing would hinder deep peace and calmness of soul from accompanying our lives.[6]

This text from the fourth century addresses a highly urgent problem in our world today. Affluence—namely, the excessive accumulation of wealth at the cost of the poor, the I-want-more attitude—has a tendency not only to result in physical overeating but also to give rise to envy, jealousy, dispute, and discord. And that, too, happens not only at the individual but also at the social and structural level.

Fasting can help us to overcome passivity and to renew hope so that we may offer our service for justice and peace. Thus, it also has a social dimension, apart from the individual, health, and spiritual dimension. But what about the political dimension?

Fasting as a Political Tool

"My religion teaches me that whenever there is a distress which one cannot remove one must fast and pray." Gandhi wrote this sentence on September 18, 1924, after violent conflicts between Hindus and Muslims.[7] He once again underwent strict fasting so that the Hindu and Muslim leaders would come to an understanding and put an end to their disputes.

Gandhi is neither the first nor the only person to use fasting as a political tool. But as few others have, he made a very clear distinction between "Satyagraha fasting" (fasting as a nonviolent campaign) and the usually employed hunger strike. According to Gandhi, fasting as a nonviolent action requires a great purity of the heart and independence from its outcomes. For Gandhi, political fasting is another form of praying and cannot be separated from the religious dimension.

In what follows, I would like to mention two examples of such fasting. The first comes from ancient Jewish history, namely the book of Esther; the other example comes from a group of Chilean refugees. Incidentally, both examples also enlighten the complexity of fasting and how politically oriented fasting indeed contains the other dimensions of fasting; even the cosmetic aspect has its rightful place in fasting.

The Example of Esther

In short, the book of Esther tells the story of the young Jewish girl Esther, who rescues the Jews from a planned extermination, by courageously going to the Persian king Artaxerxes. For the decisive meeting with the king, she prepares together with her people by fasting for three days, saying to them, "Go, gather together all the Jews that are present in Shushan, and fast ye for me, and neither eat nor drink three days, night or day: I also and my maidens will fast likewise; and so will I go in unto the king, which is not according to the law: and if I perish, I perish" (Esther 4:16). Esther succeeds in changing the king's mind. The enemies of the Jews are exterminated, and Esther is made the queen. She celebrates the victory with her people as a festive day, the Purim festival; everybody eats and drinks and distributes gifts. Sadness is transformed into joy, fasting into celebration.

This, in short, is the story of Esther. But how does it speak to our concerns? First, there is the fact that also during these early times Jews prepared for trials and prosecutions by fasting, individually as well as in community. Also historically validated are celebrations after victories and the corresponding festivals with joyous meals, distribution of gifts, and the giving of alms to the poor. After all, the carnival-like festivities with elements of the Babylonian New Year celebration, which the Jews got to know during exile, go way back in history.

The book of Esther, written in 300 BCE, borrows these as well as other elements, combines them into a whole, and gives them a new meaning. The result is a fascinating book, which is reminiscent of the stories from the *Arabian Nights*. It does not provide an accurate record of events but gives a lively, graphic explanation of the Purim festival and Purim fasting, which was customary already at that early time.

It is interesting to note that, in the original Hebrew version of the book of Esther, God is not mentioned. It is the Greek version, which was written in about 120 BCE, which adds a theological dimension. One might read this as an attempt to "sanction" fasting in the then traditional sense, that is, to sanctify it. Religiously motivated fasting presupposes seasonal fasting as inspired by nature and politically motivated fasting.

In conclusion, we might ask, what in fact saved Esther and her people? Was it the negotiation skills of the young queen? Or her shining beauty augmented by fasting? Or the equanimity and courage produced by fasting and prayer? The answer surely lies in the integration of all these elements.

What pertains to the Purim fast and feast basically applies to every genuine fasting and feasting. *Present and past* come together: thus the annual fasting and celebrating whenever again nature awakens and points back to the communal memory of a prehistoric mythical event and one or more related persons. *Individuals and superseding community* are also joined: when fasting that pushes the individual to his or her limits is practiced by many in preparation for the feast, it strengthens the community. Likewise, *politics and religion* are linked: when fasting is intensified by prayer, it becomes a tool of liberation from an adversary (politics) or from evil (religion).

It is this integration of different, seemingly contradictory elements that comprises the power of the book of Esther, including the fasting that plays a central role in it.

The Chilean Refugees

It happened nearly a quarter-century ago in Zurich, Switzerland. I asked two bypassers the way to St. Mark's Church. Their reply: "Oh yeah, the Chileans! Straight ahead, then make a right." "The Chileans" were twenty-two women and men from Chile, scheduled to be deported from Switzerland. The Reformed Protestant Church had offered them refuge in this church. They had been fasting for more than fourteen days, to strengthen their request for asylum. In front of the church was an information stand featuring newspaper clippings and a list with names of well-known citizens vouching for the refugees. They are the names of people and were also otherwise willing to get involved.

On the door of the church, there was a page with the text, "If a foreigner lives in your country, you should not oppress him. The foreigner staying with you should be accepted as one of the locals and you should love him as you love yourself" (Leviticus 19:33–34). And on the floor at the entrance, "Hide those who have been chased away, do not betray the refugees" (Isaiah 16:3).

At 6 p.m., prayer service began. The inside of the church was pleasantly warm. This was good, since fasting easily makes one feel cold. Young people sat scattered across the large room. Both Swiss and Chileans sat together. There were also some older people. I asked a Chilean woman how she was feeling. "Not good, my head hurts," she said and moved to the front.

In the choir and in the fashion of romance countries, many candles flickered, set up to form the words "Faith in You." Psalm 127 was uttered—"Help comes to me from the LORD, who made heaven and earth"— followed by Matthew's account on the multiplication of bread and fish. Jesus' disciples were worried that there would not be enough food to feed everyone. But after Jesus' words, "Give them food yourselves," all had eaten their fill. A volunteer from the Christian Peace Service explained the text.

He asked, "But what about tiny Switzerland? Do we have work for all, food for all, shelter for all, schools for all . . . ?" And then, after a pause, "Why shouldn't the miracle happen today when we share?"

And sharing it was. A lady brought gloves for Juan, who was very thin and certainly freezing. The leader of the service let us know that earlier a man had handed him an envelope with two thousand Swiss francs. An old lady sent five thousand francs saying she was too old to be giving more.

Intercessions were brought forward, accompanied by the sounds of guitars, the answer being projected onto the old walls with an overhead projector: *Misericordias Domini in aeternum cantabo*—"I will sing of the mercy of the Lord forever." How the ancient Latin language again succeeded in uniting people of different backgrounds! But more than Latin united us that night—the awareness that we are all pilgrims on this earth, we are all foreigners looking for a home.

That night I headed home in deep thought as I suddenly understood our fear of strangers. For when we become strangers to ourselves, when we feel insecure and homeless in spite of all our wealth and possessions, then we cannot possibly offer home to others.

Two days later I read in the newspaper that the Chilean refugees had ended their hunger strike—which, in my opinion, was not a "hunger strike" but a politically motivated fast. Those concerned had hope that the solidarity of Swiss and international organizations would not fail and that a humanitarian solution would be found. Refugees are still hoping for humanitarian solutions all across the world.

Fasting is not an end in itself. We cannot be concerned just about our individual health or spiritual fitness. Some of the objectives of fasting are to practice sharing, to express solidarity with those who suffer, to campaign for a more just and peaceful world, and when necessary, to gain strength for nonviolent resistance.

4

Fasting: Why Not?

There are a lot of good reasons *for* fasting. Yet I hear many pretexts for *not* fasting. These might include the following.

"I Think That Fasting Is *Good*, but I Don't Have the Time and Peace of Mind for It"

While fasting may make sense to us, it seems unimaginable to find the necessary time, quiet, focus, strength, and motivation for it.

Yet if we take a closer look, the contrary is true: often it is the too much, our excessive and unhealthy diets, that literally "weighs us down" and prevents us from finding deeper peace of mind. What we need is to break the vicious circle, which Claude Régamey so aptly described: "Most people are caught in a vicious circle. They do not fast as they do not have the drive or enthusiasm to fast and they do not have enthusiasm or drive because they do not fast."[1]

"Why Fast? Life Is Already Difficult Enough and, Moreover, I Fear the Consequences"

This argument also can easily be refuted. Every aspect of human growth holds thresholds that cause us anxiety. This fear of the unknown exists also in fasting. It is the feeling of uncertainty when changing one's life. This is how one participant in a fasting session put it: "For a long time, I believed that this workshop was not meant for me. I was afraid that I would not enjoy cigarettes anymore." What a convincing argument *for* fasting! It takes only a little more effort to overcome this "fear of the unknown"; yet it might appear insurmountable until we try it.

A healthy lifestyle marked by temporary abstinence need not imply a drop in the quality of life. On the contrary, it helps us discover more pleasures in food and in life in general.

"Fasting Is Good, Charity Is Better"

When using this argument, people might reference the biblical text of Isaiah 58, which we discussed in the previous chapter. According to this approach, fasting means to fight injustice, to abstain from slandering others, and to share our food with the hungry. But it does not necessarily mean doing away with food. Régamey calls this "a very modern distortion." It is not a matter of *either-or* but of *and*: fasting *and* active charity. Because it is precisely the process of fasting that makes us more open and more sensitive to the plight of others. What Isaiah means is this: it is not fasting in and by itself that is praiseworthy and pleases God; it is the fasting that leads us to active compassion.

"I've Heard the Message, Yet I Lack the Courage"

At times, the state of dwindling religious faith today is associated with the end of fasting. But this is questionable. Which faith and which fasting are we talking about? If one is speaking of old church laws and compulsory fasting, this observation is justified. Fasting as religious obligation is rarely practiced today. But if this faith is a free, living relationship with the deeper meaning of our existence or, for Christians, a relationship with Jesus Christ who himself found his call when fasting, then it is fasting that is capable of substantiating our faith.

Learning faith through fasting—learning fasting in faith! Try it. But do not feel pressured by either of them. Faith, just like fasting, draws its power from the depths of the heart, which is sacrosanct in its freedom.

If you want to give fasting, like faith, a—or another—try, then let the love of silence be your first step. The next step would be the love for your higher self or, if you like, the love for your personal calling. And if you are Christian, your love for Christ will show you the way and stand you in good measure.

Fasting: Well, Why Not?

Yes, why not? And if you have further questions about the when and how of fasting, and if you are looking for encouragement from the testimonies of others, then I invite you to continue reading this book.

Part II

How to Fast

When you suffer fasting instead of mastering it you will collapse into yourself, become depressed, and break out into cold sweats. Breathing gets stuck. The heart shudders. The voice becomes hoarse and the head feels empty. But if you remain strong, ultimately you will discover an energy beyond the limits of your own energy.

—Lanza del Vasto

To fast or to "be fasted," that is the question. When we are willing to go the inner path, when we understand the deeper perspectives and learn the fasting process and what steps need to be observed—moreover, when others share their experiences with the healthful practice of fasting, their joys and pains and how it helped them grow—then we will lose our fears and fast with greater energy. Rather than being an object, we will become the subject of the event, we will create our own fasting and, in the process, learn to eat with greater awareness.

© Mikael Damkier - Fotolia.com

5

Fasting Can Be Learned

We say that where there is a will, there is a way. This is true but not always helpful. The reverse also holds true: where there is a way, there is a will. In this sense, I understand the following points as guidelines. The explanations in part 1 validate these guidelines and they presuppose that you have read those earlier chapters.

Who Can Fast and Who Should Not?

A person is never too young and seldom too old to fast. A fourteen-year-old, if grown and mature enough, may fast. And those who are used to fasting can undergo this salutary treatment even at the age of eighty or more, provided there are no medical reasons prohibiting it.

Fasting can be beneficial to the following conditions: certain kinds of heart disease, arthritis, asthma, diseases of the digestive system, diabetes due to obesity, malfunctions of the liver and pancreas, skin diseases, migraines, and even anorexia.

Anorexia is especially common among young girls and may be caused by a resistance to physical-sexual maturing. This psychologically caused refusal to eat requires careful psychotherapy, but some have found that fasting can be a successful part of treatment. This is not surprising if you consider that fasting brings about a new positive attitude to food and the experience of one's physical being.

Another frequently asked question is whether fasting is advisable for people who suffer from conditions such as manic depression, epilepsy, or schizophrenia. As long as appropriate medical care is provided, fasting is possible. In fact, astonishing success stories exist, and certain kinds of depressions can be relieved after just one fast. Quite obviously, in the case of any present illness, fasting should take place only in suitable clinics under strict medical supervision.

But there are also *contraindications* for fasting—conditions and factors that increase its risks—for instance, all degenerative diseases such as tuberculosis, gout, cancer, senility, as well as certain medical therapies. The decisive question is always whether the body is robust enough to respond to the strong impulse of fasting. Therefore, one's general health and good spirits carry more weight than might an actual organic disease.

Yet, not only the sick but also the healthy benefit from fasting. Otto Buchinger dared to hope that the next generation—namely, us—would set up several fasting homes in every area, one for the sick and three or four for healthy fasters. As Buchinger wrote, "The so-called healthy person should fast. Sincere annual fasting should protect from illness and infirmity. One should not wait until the forerunners of death, the diseases, take hold."

Fasting Alone or Fasting Together?

When you are healthy (consult your doctor!), somewhat rested, and when you know the basic rules of fasting and, more importantly, of breaking a fast, and when perhaps you have the guidance of a doctor or experienced fasting guide, then you may venture into fasting independently, at least for a few days. But generally speaking, unaccompanied fasting is as little recommended as climbing a mountain without joining a rope team or without the guidance of people who already know the way. Over three decades ago, Dr. Claude Régamey called for "experienced men, priest-doctors, gurus" who experience fasting anew and under diverse circumstances. Increasingly, such men and women exist and offer guided fasting. Most important in a fasting guide is the ability to lead others to a genuine motivation and help them to fast as subjects who responsibly shape their own experience.

When to Fast

Spring is favorable for fasting since this is the time when nature reawakens. Thus, it is not without reason that most religions have their ritual fasting during this time. But this does not mean that other seasons are not favorable. The *Legenda Aurea* (*The Golden Legend*), the widely read religious chapbook of the Middle Ages, enumerates not less than eight reasons why we should fast in all the four seasons, though they may sound peculiar to the modern reader. For example,

> The sixth point is that spring is like air, and thus we fast against the thin air of vanity. Summer is like fire, and thus we fast against the heat of desire. Autumn is like earth and thus we fast against the cold of spiritual frigidity and against ignorance. Winter is like water, and thus we fast against the buoyant flow and restlessness of our mind. The seventh point is that spring is like childhood, summer like youth, autumn like middle age and winter like old age. Thus, when we fast in spring, we are like innocent children; in summer we are like steadfast youth; in autumn we mature with modesty and discipline and in winter, we become old with wisdom and a respectable life.[1]

Every season can therefore contribute to making fasting a memorable experience: spring with its growing and regenerating nature; summer with its sun baths, air baths, as well as water splashes; autumn being the most contemplative of all the seasons; and winter when the warmth and comfort of the house protects one from the howling storm and bitter cold outside.

When you fast in cold weather, remember that during fasting your body runs on a low-energy program. You might get cold more easily, especially in your hands and feet. Therefore, it is important to wear warmer clothes, put your feet in hot water at times, or take a hot-water bottle to bed. Even a cup of peppermint tea can be useful.

I have had good experiences with fasting in late spring and summer. Christian organizations rightfully recommend the time before Easter, that is, Lent (the "fasting time"), for this cleansing and healing exercise.

How to Begin

There are three basic phases in fasting: beginning with the process of "switching," the actual fasting, and then the breaking of the fast and a period of "rebuilding." The third phase is the most difficult phase, but the beginning can be rough as well. Before starting a fast, you may be suddenly overcome by a strange nervousness. You may want really to eat once more, and then rush through the step of bowel cleansing.

Therefore, make sure that you give yourself enough time, and give your soul a chance to keep up with your decision. Switching to inner nutrition is not a mechanical process. It needs a lot of care. It helps to anticipate your fast weeks ahead of time and to have one or two days with only raw vegetables and fruits before you begin fasting. Then on the first day you would take six tablespoons of salt, dissolved in one to two glasses of warm water or with chamomile tea, to help empty your bowels. (Also, review chapter 1 on what happens in the process of "switching.")

What Is Important During the Fast

The actual fasting is the easiest of the three phases, for we can safely entrust ourselves to the intelligence of our body. Nevertheless, it is helpful to pay special attention to the following factors, especially if you have not had prior experience.

Adjusting to a Different Rhythm

When fasting, it helps to adapt to the slower rhythm of your body, and, in general, to become aware of what does your body well. In any case, make sure that you do not get up too fast; take time to stretch, then sit a moment on the edge of the bed before standing up. This will avoid feelings of dizziness and nausea. When you continue work while fasting, take a rest and relax a bit when others are eating. Even a carpeted floor can be a good place for a nap.

Hygienic Measures

Since fasting is a far-reaching process of purging and excretion, being careful about one's cleanliness is very important. Exercise thorough oral hygiene and skin care; take regular showers but avoid taking hot baths.

Exercise and fresh air will likely appeal to you more than usual. It is in this context that Gandhi gave this advice: "Bathe yourself in morning air."

Every other day you will need an enema or to drink a mild laxative tea. You will be amazed how much needless or toxic stuff your body cleans out during a fast.

Supporting Detoxification

During the entire fast, make sure that you support your liver's detox work, especially at lunchtime if at all possible, when you are more likely to experience discomfort or crisis. A hot-water bottle or a liver pack—a hot humid bandage approximately eight inches wide and the height of the liver—works wonders. A massage can be of great help. And, by the way, be patient with yourself especially on so-called crisis days. It is important to know that there will be times of discomfort triggered by detoxification and the healing process that fasting initiates.

Drink Plenty of Liquids

Fasting is a detox cure, and liquids play an important role in it. Drink a lot of water—at least two quarts a day!

Supporting Routines

Etymologically, the word *fast* is connected to the word *fasten*, meaning to hold on, to retain. Thus, to fast means to hold on to rules and regulations, to pay attention to them in the sense of following a method. However, the objective of all rules and regulations is freedom, not slavish subjugation. As psychotherapist Rüdiger Dahlke very aptly puts it, if during your twenty-fifth fast you still obsess about recipes and instructions, you are like a swimmer who, out of habit, even after twenty years, does not want to give up the buoyancy belt.[2]

As far as fasting is concerned, we distinguish between complete fasting and partial fasting. In complete fasting, you either completely give up eating for entire days or weeks or you consume very few calories in the form of fruit and vegetable juices. Partial fasting, which is better known as "dieting," is basically reduced food intake, for instance, in the form of fruits, vegetables, or potatoes. It may at first sound surprising that complete fasting is much easier than taking in less food. But when we take a closer look, it becomes obvious. In complete fasting, our body does not "expect" anything from the outside and after switchover remains calm. In partial fasting, however, our body expects food and experiences a lack thereof, which leads to frustration. This is precisely the case both during the period of buildup to ending a fast and afterward as well. A person experienced in fasting knows how critical this last phase can be and has learned to feed both on food from the outside and continued nutrition from the body itself during this transition period. Thus the buildup time becomes much easier.

Complete fasting is done with water, tea, or, like the Buchinger method, using tea and limited fruit juices and vegetable broths. It is my own experience that the Buchinger fasting method is especially appropriate for a healing fast. Why? Offering four "meals" per day (see the fasting-liquid recipes in appendix 2) keeps it parallel to a usual meal schedule and therefore can encourage a readiness to acquire new eating habits while fasting and, in general, to engage in a transformative process integrating one's whole life.

Regarding the so-called supporting measures, Otto Buchinger found these to be even more important than the fasting itself. Above all, they include quiet time and opportunities to come to ourselves and be with ourselves. In general, fasting makes us more sensitive and receptive. It is up to us what we do with this openness and relaxation. One might, for instance, try to reorient one's life during a retreat at a spiritual or meditation center.

Pilates and yoga exercises are also recommended as supporting measures since they help us to exercise calmness and mental alertness; they can strengthen the fasting process. To a certain extent, fasting also goes well together with Zen meditation. However, a rigorous Zen practice should not be combined with fasting for various reasons, including switchover processes and other forms of "concentration."

Indeed, every form of motivation that favors the holistic approach of fasting is helpful. It is also an experience that a fasting "for" helps us to practice solidarity with others, especially with those who suffer, and thus can help us to get over the minor complaints and crises that fasting presents. As I mentioned earlier, my experiences of fasting in community for justice, peace, and the preservation of the universe have been very encouraging.

How to Complete a Fast and Why to Repeat

It is most important to adhere to the following rules when ending a fast after a few days or after longer periods if you are experienced enough and under medical supervision.

The buildup period should take at least one-third of the fasting time. For example, a fast of twelve days requires a buildup of three to four days. The change from fasting back to eating reaches deep into our physical and psychological constitution. Don't be surprised if you experience fatigue, a feeling of being overweight, pain in the joints, reluctance to work, and so forth. Buildup may even come with feelings of a slight depression. However, when following buildup rules (see the list in the appendix) the careless, light mood of the fasting days returns swiftly.

If you continue fasting regularly, if possible once a year, your body will find it easy to switch from external nutrition to internal nutrition. It is as if regaining our long-lost and nearly completely forgotten ability to go through winter hibernating or, indeed, fasting.

The physiological processes will then not be as strenuous and we will become more open to the deeper psychosomatic, spiritual, and social dimensions of fasting.

Repetition makes fasting easier and more interesting, and that is important. An exercise like fasting that challenges all our forces doesn't go well with compulsion or disenchantment. The results will show it; inspiration of the heart and an inexplicable joy are a trademark of repeated authentic fasting. Therefore, make sure not to forget to be happy when fasting or, better yet, to fast in ways that allow you to discover how fasting creates pure joy.

6

Fasting Experiences

At the end of a fourteen-day meditation course along with a fasting period, I invited the participants to write a reflection on their experience for this book. This is what I told them: Write one or two pages sharing what you find to be interesting to others who want to understand the effects of meditating and fasting.

Nine of these reports I include here, from four women and five men between the ages of thirty-seven and sixty-two years. In order to retain the personal style and manner of writing, these reports were left unchanged except for a few minor cuts. I also did not categorize or structure them in any way.

"I Feel Like a Completely New Person"

I start this course with a lot of idealism and goodwill, knowing that I am also doing something beneficial for my health. Happily we eat our last apple. But the first days are disappointing: headaches, aching joints, a bad back, confusing thoughts, and unsuccessful attempts at mindful breathing during meditations. The longer I sit still, the more restless I become inwardly—just now, when all this is meant to help me compose myself, look inward, and become free. This gives rise to doubts. Did I choose this course for egoistic reasons, simply as an ego trip? I have left behind people at home and work, possibly letting someone down. And all this for what? Am I on the right path?

After an extremely difficult phase of settling in and an intensive assessment of my doubts, I have more profound experiences and I realize that this exercise requires of me a lot of patience and humility. I understand in body and soul: As long as there is still a trace of ambition to want to use this time, as long as I anxiously seek contemplation, I will drive away all. So I tell myself, just accept humbly whatever unfinished business appears, whatever thoughts and observations catch your attention. After all, this is what you have been practicing for years as a psychologist. But now you must give yourself some time to "unlearn the learned."

The course is over and I am filled with gratitude that I got through—sat through the fasting period in meditation. Also, I am grateful for the experience of community where everybody abides, without words. My senses, refined by fasting, silence, meditation, and the physical processes involved, perceive personal and suprapersonal realities in ways I hadn't known. I now feel myself anew as part of the whole cosmos. Nothing has changed but everything is different.

It is difficult to express this inner experience in words. Yet this entire process has made me a stronger person and hopefully also a lot more balanced and humble than when I embarked upon this journey. I look forward to the challenges of my daily life. The first thing I want to do is to cook asparagus, sip a bit of wine, and chat with friends.

As to the future, I would like to be a part of this spiritual exercise at least once a year if possible: fasting for reasons of solidarity with those on this earth who are starving; fasting as an attempt to attain moderation at a time when the world is full of suffering due to thoughtless consumption and abundance; fasting as an exercise to give away a part of our own selves.

"I Felt Fully Alive"

I have fasted four times before this and plan to do so again next year. When I ask myself why I fast, what these annual fourteen days of retreat are good for, I find these reasons: First, my health. When I was a little boy, I suffered a nearly fatal food poisoning that left lasting effects on my body. These days of revival are the best gift I can give my body.

Second, there are mental and spiritual reasons. For a while I leave behind my work and all related activities in order to center myself. Each time, this encounter with myself has turned out to be an adventure that nevertheless brings me closer to myself. In addition, fasting apparently strengthens my senses, and mental and spiritual capacities to actively perceive my surroundings and live through my days. The following notes from my diary show how comforting this whole experience was:

Fifth day of fasting: During the sixteen hours of this day, I thought of food only four times and only because the words *tea* and *refreshments* on the schedule for the day reminded me of it. So far I have not felt hungry, at least not worth mentioning. The vegetable stock seasoned with herbs and the fresh spring water served at noon were delicious. I wondered, am I expecting less or has my sensation of taste improved? I have become very receptive and grateful for my senses. A glass of water seems like a gift to me and, come to think of it, it truly is a gift of life.

Tenth day of fasting: Today I woke up at 5:30 a.m. and felt quite active. I was already back from a short walk when wake-up music echoed through the building. The melodies entered my body, inadvertently I began to exercise—an enthusiastic combination of dance, aerobics, and ski workout. I felt very comfortable. This isn't only because of the lost weight. This feeling of happiness is more profound—I feel connected to all living creatures in this world and I yearn to include my wife, kids, and all my companions here and elsewhere into this living experience. Today, a creative thought crossed my mind: from now on, I will assess all my work activities on the basis of how much they support my life.

Twelfth day of fasting: I am on my daily one-hour hike. (This walk is not a part of the program; I do it on my own.) The lower part of the route is steep. Nevertheless, my pace stays almost always the same. Fasting has not reduced my physical strength. I feel light and exceptionally well and while walking I try to be mindful of my breathing into the lower abdomen. As I walk step by step from this center of my breathing, suddenly a spiritual thought emerges from the silence, Jesus' words: "I am the way . . ."

Why would I want to repeat this particular fasting meditation? Foremost, I get to experience silence here. A few years back, I visited a fasting course at another place that was far from silent.

The participants talked about food, feasts, and culinary delights for hours and raved on about the culinary pleasures that they would relish after the fasting course was over. In such an environment, many people had problems sticking to their fasting regime. However, this same fasting experience can be completely different when it is coupled with silence and meditation. Food cravings disappear quickly, and you get a sense of inner peace, which leaves room for more.

Also important to me has been the fact that all physical, mental, and spiritual experiences become more intense for me during the silence of this fast. Maybe I fast because then I enjoy a more intense living. Freed from the constant flow of information I become more sensitive to basic and apparently natural values and I open up to creative impulses and energies that I can then bring back into my daily life.

"I Learned That Sacrifice Does Not Always Mean Loss"

For the last twenty years, the annual fasting for me meant "butter and honey." One could think I am addicted to fasting. But my only addictions are the daily, simple, yet tasty snacks that I take in during the year and that assimilate into extra body weight.

Nevertheless, I wouldn't spend fourteen precious days of my life in sacrifice just for these meager seven or eight pounds—which I will not be taking back with me after this fasting exercise—were there not other rewards from this fasting.

Reining in my appetite or, more appropriately said, my food addiction and proving to myself that I am (still) capable of forgoing things voluntarily gives me a really good feeling.

"Sacrifice does not always mean loss," my psychology professor used to say, a statement that, despite my enthusiasm for this teacher, seemed unacceptable then. Since then I certainly have experienced the truth of those words. And certainly it holds true for fasting, even though it seems difficult to prove. What would be my physical condition today without this annual cleanout? I am also convinced without being able to prove it that I owe my health, my spiritual balance (however much I have at least), my mental sharpness, and my physical fitness to this regular and systematic abstinence from my beloved food. I hardly dare speak much about the mental-spiritual experiences during fasting; this is for others to discern. Just this: such truth and clarity of mind I do not experience during the rest of the year.

An Executive's Thoughts on Fasting

I was sitting with a group of colleagues during lunch. I casually told them about my forthcoming retreat. There was a bit of curiosity at first and then the question, "Where are you going? It is winter; are you going skiing?"

Surprise was evident on their faces when I tried to explain why I wanted to go on a fast, to meditate and be silent for two weeks.

There were more questions and opinions: "You consider that a vacation?" "Do you want to lose weight?" "Is fasting a new trend, an exclusive pastime, something like golf or tennis?" "Fasting is for pious people and clerics." "The Bible talks about fasting quite often." "In more recent times, Gandhi achieved much by fasting. But he was Indian; fasting is not for us in the West."

Responding myself with a few questions—"Really? Are you sure?"—I realized that I really wasn't that convinced of my plan. But still I feel open and also a bit uneasy.

The first couple of days were tough, fear emerged whether I would be able to do this. I was tired, felt helpless, and found it difficult to concentrate. However, from the third day onward, my thoughts brighten, and quite suddenly I experience a new strength arising from within me. Suddenly all those things that seemed so important to me disappeared: my extreme ambition, strong need for entertainment, dull partying habits, continuous physical and mental commotion, and this feeling that without me nothing happens. Here things take on their appropriate importance. I recover my ability to sort through things: What is important? What takes priority over senseless activism?

Questions appear: I did not give enough time to this employee or that problem. I did not listen long enough, or I waited too long until interrupting a senseless conversation. Some people love to talk about themselves. I want to give more time to those quiet ones who nevertheless do their work extremely well without much complaining. When was the last time I had a really good conversation with my son or my daughter or even with my wife for that matter?

Indeed, this list can just go on and on. Insights take on form when we fast. We start seeing our failures honestly, without drama, and feelings of regret might come up.

During my fast I had a brief experience that keeps coming to mind. A baker drove past me on the road in his station wagon. The rear part of his vehicle was filled with delicious brown bread. That same moment I "smelled and tasted" this bread. Images from third-world countries appeared in my mind. Imaginations of how a person in such a country must feel when looking at us with hungry eyes, tired hands stretched out wearily for help. Sacrifice helps empathy, makes us more open for the plight of others.

The course is coming to its end. Will I be able to convey to my employees that I like and respect all of them and that it is all right if they make mistakes at times or do not always fulfill all their duties? Can I communicate that our work is not just about self-realization or for money making but can also serve others? Will I be able to muster the patience, energy, and consistence necessary, once I am back working with my employees daily and meeting challenges? I really hope and wish I do.

Four weeks later: It can't be hidden, I have changed. I no longer think of my work as a heavy burden, and it is no longer the only objective of my existence. I am clearly more patient with others and with myself even when it comes to tricky questions and situations. My thoughts are clearer. Sleep is more sound and deep. I haven't put on any weight again; I eat more consciously and try to avoid the "old indulgences."

I have interesting conversations with my employees and business partners as they notice changes in my behavior and ask me about it.

A Path That Continues

Saturday, Day 1: The first day of fasting is coming to an end. I ate yesterday's apple and the salt drink was in an odd way "yummy" as always.

After a short afternoon nap, I took a short walk up the nearby hill; it is still there. And I met a couple of old acquaintances.

Tuesday, Day 4: I'm back. I got over yesterday's thoughts: "No normal person would do anything as stupid as this." Yet I had been looking forward to come back here for the entire past year.

But now I can see the light at the end of the tunnel. I ask myself, do I really want a change? When has there ever been a change without a crisis?

Friday, Day 7: Today is the seventh day. It should have been a day of crisis, but I feel nothing like it. Every day is a good day. All that fatigue of the past days has vanished. My handwriting is dynamic and I like it. I did not sleep soundly last night but then I used that wakeful time, or if I may say, I enjoyed it.

I feel that now I can be centered and dynamic at the same time. Apparently, habits developed over time can change. I am hopeful.

Yesterday was Ms. B's birthday. Two glorious bouquets of flowers adorn the entrance hall. What fragrance! I also notice the pictures in the hall and the birds outside with great intensity. And the same is true for people. I am aware of a lot more than usual. I remember this from earlier fasts. I become more loving and tolerant, yet at times also more direct and critical toward others.

Monday, Day 10: A scar on my stomach from an operation forty years ago makes its presence felt once more. But this time is different. I feel energy flowing into this area, blood circulation increases.

In general, my blood circulation is changing. After the first two fasting retreats, I returned home

© John Hemmings - Fotolia.com

with an almost whitish-grey complexion. Since child-hood I had always been pale. Since the third course, a year ago, the blood circulation around my face has improved a lot.

My knees are much better; in the past walking downhill produced a lot of pain in my knees. And my frequent headaches, which used to start right from the back of my neck, have almost disappeared over the years.

Tuesday, Day 11: This night I wrote a long letter to my daughter. Until now I didn't want to interfere in her life, but yesterday it suddenly stood out so clear to me: here you have to help her make a sound decision. I am amazed how active I am during this fast.

Wednesday, Day 12: I just ate the first apple after my fast. It is really the best meal when breaking the fast. All is peaceful. I am eating like I have always wanted to eat—enjoying every bit of it. A good exercise. Fasting for me is *the* opportunity to practice controlled eating.

And vice versa: controlled eating is a prepara-tion for fasting. Together it becomes a way to practice inner freedom, the ability to do something or to let it be when I believe that is the right thing to do.

Thursday, Day 13: Breakfast today offers a bit to chew. In the afternoon we will talk once more. This time I didn't weigh myself, I will check when getting home, I expect to have lost around nine pounds.

Friday, Day 14: I met a few interesting people today. It is remarkable how relaxed people have become with other after sharing this two-week experience, yet hardly speaking a word with each other.

I will soon turn sixty and most of the opportunities of my life lie behind me. But I do not like getting into a deadlock—somehow, somewhere life must go on. For me, fasting and meditation open the doors to a path that never ends.

Fasting: A Special Type of Fitness Training

A few years back, I attended a lecture on fasting by a doctor who was the head of a fasting clinic. I was amazed to learn about the positive effects fasting has on our health. In particular I was impressed by a story an elderly woman shared in the question-and-answer session following the lecture. She described her annual three-week fasts and how she continues working in her garden and taking long walks every day during that period of time.

After the lecture, I bought *The New Life Fasting Book* by Dr. Luetzner, a medically inspired guide for independent fasting. After reading this easily understandable and well-written book, my decision was clear.

I wanted to give fasting a try, simply to detoxify my body and to lose some weight. Starting out with great enthusiasm I encountered my first challenge when drinking the salt drink. My body, taking the salt as an insult, cleaned itself out—quite effectively—the wrong way by making me throw up. Therefore, I developed a strong aversion against the salt and decided on another way to empty out my bowels, namely by adding a day of eating just raw fruit and vegetables. This was followed by a glass of sauerkraut juice and a glass of warm mineral water, and an occasional enema during the fast.

The following seven fasting days proved to me how surprisingly easy it was not to eat. After my midday vegetable juice I also went out for walks. This was something I had been planning for quite some time but had never managed to actually do. I felt really good!

However, I made a lot of mistakes during the buildup period after the fast and as a result soon was back to my original weight. Nevertheless, I had learned a lot:

- Fasting is much easier for me than eating less.
- During the fast I was much more balanced and my reactions to discomfort were less aggressive than usual.
- The excessive sensitivity of my facial skin to artificial foodstuffs and environmental influences calmed down considerably after fasting.
- Even after long workdays, I felt a lot fresher and more active.
- I became a much more attentive listener.

I suddenly felt motivated to fast for a longer duration and under guidance, and thus registered for this retreat.

I had a lot of expectations; primarily I hoped to discover the purpose of my life, away from the usual distractions.

It was especially pleasant that the retreat didn't as much focus on the fasting as it stressed the opportunity to encounter the self and to experience how encouraging it is to fast together with others.

Today, after three weeks of fasting, I feel like I have been attending a kind of fitness training. I not only feel stronger, more energetic, and less lazy physically, but I have also managed to get down to doing things that I kept putting off for months. What amazes and delights me is that I feel a trusting connection with others who fasted with me without knowing them or even having spoken with them, something that does not come naturally to me.

I want to do an occasional fast "on my own," and then want to follow a few guidelines I didn't know during my first fasting experiences:

- In order to prevent dizziness when getting up in the morning (especially in case of low blood pressure), it helps to first stretch properly, massage the back of your feet, and always to keep a glass of water within your reach.
- Plan for extra time between getting up and going out of the house.
- During the fasting period, do not discuss fasting with people who have never experienced it so that you do not get distracted by their apprehensions, fears, or admiration.
- Avoid the news and other mass media, since during fasting impressions are much more vivid and can result in nightmares.

- Keep a fasting diary to record how you feel, what you do, what changes, and so forth.
- Avoid invitations and celebrations during the fast, but certainly and during the buildup period.

The Biggest Surprise

On the first evening I was chewing the obligatory apple, reflecting upon the moment. This was going to be my last solid food for a long time. I was suddenly doubtful: Will I be up to the fast? What if hunger plagues me and "I just cannot take it any longer"? I admired my own courage for registering for the retreat and tried to calm myself down by saying that at least meditation and silence were not new to me. Yes, meditation was actually the main reason why I decided to do this course—meditation for long periods of time intensified by a potential fasting experience.

Today, two weeks after the retreat, I am reading my diary with awe and with a smile on my face. It concludes, "Fasting turned out to be a huge surprise for me. Before starting this course, I saw myself going through these fourteen days with a firm determination and a grumbling stomach. But it did not turn out to be like that at all. Except for the fourth day (palpitations/breaking out into a sweat just before noon), I did not face any problems. Not just that, I felt absolutely normal."

During the following days, I felt increasingly aware and grateful for everything—the past, the present, and the future, all that was given to me, which I could experience and become mindful of; and everything related to a greater power, to the cosmos, and the divine. Was it because of meditation or fasting? I believe both. This is what I had written in my diary:

> *11th day:* Despite the silence I feel a growing connection with others present here. I feel clearly that concerns and problems are carried by the entire group. We have been silent together for a good ten days and yet everyone is getting to know each other. This is something utterly surprising to me for somehow, we are all connected to each other just like mountains and ridges which proudly rise above the fog yet share a common base. . . . One certain success I had in my meditation. I could sit without any problems for the last ten days. This allowed me to work more on my sitting posture. I also learned that I can concentrate on my breathing really only when sitting correctly.

A Longer Fast Resulted in a More Profound Experience

Eleven years back, I went on a water fast for a week. Words from the Christian liturgy provoked me to do so: "Fasting helps you suppress sin, elevate your spirit, and increase the strength of your virtue." I experienced days of serenity, concentration, and calm as if being a child again. It was a beginner's fast but I came to like it and since have fasted every year. In addition to losing a few pounds, it has also cured an ugly migraine. I took back the weight after only a few days because I did not know much about the right methods of breaking a fast and the buildup period. However, the migraine has never since troubled me. In the following years, I fasted during all my vacations and always came out of it feeling calmer, fresher and ready for the tasks that lay ahead. Fasting also made my vacations simpler and cheaper.

Later I tried to fast in solitude and noted in my diary, "I want to make my life simpler, give up on a few habits, and I want to develop eating, living, and praying habits which can accompany me into old age, and hold me even in a possibly lonesome old age: not anymore chasing stuff through my head, heart, and stomach, but finding a path for giving myself to life."

Francis of Assisi (the founder of our religious congregation) fasted for forty days on Isola Maggiore on Lake Trasimeno in Italy. When I once did the same for eight days, I wrote in my diary, "My dreams reveal to me a tendency to show off, I am seeing myself performing ski acrobatics, worthy of winning me a freestyle championship."

Once I had a beautiful experience when visiting with another monk from my order, who is a hermit. He had awaited me with great mindfulness, and welcomed me warmly. He took my backpack, offered me a cube of sugar soaked in liquor as a refreshment (customary with the farmers in the vicinity), then attached thin stripes of fur to my skis for the last part of the journey. And for days on end, there was nothing stronger than the presence of the great and humble God in the almost total silence of the snowed-in mountains and in the powerful silence of the Eucharist. This presence, this being there, this attending amid dire fatigue, amid the darkness, amid the depths and chasms, amid great joy and the simplicity of the ordinary; this patient awaiting inherent in all human existence, this waiting for God has ever since with its gracious charm drawn me to fasting.

Then I attended my first fourteen-day retreat here. I noticed how deep-lying deposits in my body and soul were tackled. And now I am on a four-week fast, and I am happy to be back here. More clearly than ever do I feel a tendency to hold on to a truth, a virtue, a balanced beauty. Especially thanks to the mediation work I become more able to let go. And this: Nothing is forlorn and I am not at all left alone. Rarely have I been so secluded and yet so connected. Relationships develop. Simply. Through one basic bond.

In the coming spring, I want to fast for forty days. The director of this retreat, Fr. Brantschen, believes that I am capable of this. "Motivation is crucial," he told me. Ambition harms the proposition.

"Thanks to Fasting, I'm Happy to Be a Mensch"

I find it difficult to put into words my experience of fasting. I think that since every person is different, everybody's fasting experience is also different. In addition, I experience each fast in a very different way.

The physical discomforts caused by fasting have never created any real problems for me. At the beginning, I experience a bit of nausea, headache, fatigue, and a few other pains and aches. But soon I feel physically more agile, and more relaxed than usual. And I realize ever more clearly how important a certain practice is, regular discipline, healthy eating habits and daily exercise if we want to experience the unity of body and soul.

For the spiritual and mental areas, I compare my fasting to the theme of Beethoven's Fifth Symphony: "Thus destiny knocks at the door." Serenity, silence, and staying gathered all help me to go deeper. Love for God, love for the other being, love for nature all grow: I look differently on every flower, every grass, even on an annoying little fly. During these times of fasting I hear the chirping of birds as a special message often ignored in everyday life. The meaningful combination of fasting, meditation, work on the body (posture exercises), prayer, and lectures helps me to open up, and again and again I am astounded simply by being, being me just as I am.

At the same time, this transparency also makes me see and experience some painful thorns. The common focus in the group helps to get through times of crisis.

Once I return to my regular life I feel an inexpressible source of strength, live life to the fullest, feel difficulties and beauty more intensively; it becomes easier for me to recognize what is important and right, and I feel happy to be a "mensch"—fully human, in the best sense of the word.

7

Fasting and Silence

Fasting is primarily an issue of solitude and silence, according to Otto Buchinger, the renowned pioneer of healing through fasting. The time of fasting becomes for us, he said, "a eternal minute of silence in our hectic life."[1] Fasting and silence are as interlinked as breathing in and breathing out. One cannot exist without the other. But what exactly do we mean by silence?[2] How does this silence influence fasting and how does fasting lead to a silence that is more than just the absence of words?

The Silence We Mean

Serenity and silence! We are strangely ambivalent about these qualities. They attract us and at the same time deter us; we long for them, yet we are afraid to expose ourselves to them. One of the reasons is that, when silent, we encounter ourselves, including our shadow sides, our unresolved problems, and the things we've hidden even from our own eyes. We are similarly ambivalent about fasting. A man once told me very seriously that fasting is not his cup of tea. He was afraid that he would then no longer be able to enjoy a cigarette.

But fasting is a risk worth taking—as much as the risk (or the opportunity!) to practice and experience serenity and profound silence as something far reaching, corrective, and guiding. In his outstanding work *The World of Silence*, Max Picard expresses this thought as follows: "Silence will look upon man everywhere. Silence sees man more than man sees it. Man does not test silence, but silence tests man."[3]

Silence Favors Fasting

The importance of silence for fasting has already been mentioned in the previous chapter's personal reports from those who have gone through a fast. Indeed, I cannot imagine a significant fast that does not give importance to silence. The great spiritual traditions made retreat and silence a part of fasting. The rattle of *Carneval* (Latin for "good-bye meat") must cease for fasting to begin.

Otto Buchinger rediscovered this age-old knowledge, though it was only after many years of experience that he understood more clearly the intimate connection between silence and fasting. Toward the end of his life he understood the so-called supportive methods, such as healing life coaching, "moral encouragement," and the cultivation of silence, as the main dimension of fasting.[4] Buchinger thus provided a continuing impulse for holistic and spiritually motivated fasting.

Fasting Deepens Silence

Silence and fasting are interdependent. Serenity and the practice of silence give vigor to a fast; and in turn,

© Nicola Vernizzi - Fotolia.com

fasting deepens silence. This is linked to the change-over process that we have already discussed. A mindful changeover from external nutrition to internal nutrition initiates a process of interiorization. People who fast correctly, that is, from a wholesome motivation, will develop a natural need to turn toward their inner selves, to retain their body heat and manage their energies sensibly. This in turn favors retreat and silence.

During a fast we can experience what philosopher Max Picard said about the power of silence. When we practice silence while fasting—for example, through meditation methods—we intensify this experience. We begin to understand the incomprehensible, to see the invisible and to touch within a fulfilled moment the far ends of eternity. As Picard wrote, "Silence is not visible, but it exists. It extends into all distance and yet is close to us, so close that we can feel it like our own body. We cannot grab it but sense it directly like a fabric, a weaving. We cannot define it by words, but it is definite and unmistakeable."[5] All these things clearly indicate that fasting and silence go hand in hand. They depend on each other and also intensify each other's effects. However, what if a fast is not done within the protective walls of a retreat center or a specialty clinic? What are the basic things that should be observed when fasting in everyday life? This is what we explore in the next chapter.

8

Fasting in Everyday Life

The word *fasting* might make us think of a clinic or doctors, of the seclusion of a retreat house, or at least of a vacation. Rarely do we relate fasting to daily routine and work. Is it possible to fast during ordinary days? Yes, it is, but under certain conditions. If these conditions are followed, fasting not only becomes possible in everyday life but also proves to be an experience that is unlike anything that can be obtained in seclusion.

If you want to fast in everyday life, make sure you observe the following things. Do not select a time for fasting when you are going to be under tremendous work pressure or have a lot of social commitments. The question here is not really whether or not you can deal with your work pressures. The question is whether you can manage to take out sufficient time from your hectic schedules for self-reflection, for instance, in the evenings or during the weekend. This self-reflection is necessary for being able to enjoy the complete experience of fasting. Ask yourself the following questions:

- What does my work schedule look like before, during, and after the fasting week? Can I take a day off in case problems arise? There can be occasional concentration problems during a zero-calorie fast. Therefore, activities that involve great responsibility and require complete concentration, such as driving a vehicle, operating heavy machinery, and the like, should not be practiced when fasting.
- When I am working, can I take an extended lunch break to fulfill the need for peace and self-reflection?
- What are my plans with my family and during free time in this week? Does my family approve of my plans?

When we fast, support from the people we live with is extremely important. I know of a few women who did not want to take part in a daily group fast only because they feared that their partners would laugh at them. However, mutual understanding between the partners or several family members—for instance, parents and older children—fasting together can help create an ideal atmosphere for the practice as well as establish a new eating pattern afterward. I have often heard of mothers who fast but do not mind cooking for others.

Just as helpful is the support of others who are also fasting. In addition to sharing the experience, such a group should offer a space for reflection on the different

aspects of fasting—health related, spiritual, and social—
so that the fasting can become a wholesome experience
also during ordinary days.

The experience of the time after a fast, the buildup
period, I have found is just as good in everyday fasts
as it is during retreat fasting. Why? Because, when
fasting in everyday life, "returning to daily routine" is
easier since one has forgone only the food and not the
daily routine.

When asked about their postfasting experience
during a gathering held after the completion of the
fasting period, participants of group fasting in everyday life said the following:

- When fasting in everyday life, I learned to eat slower;
  I started having more apples and muesli and less
  coffee. I decided to keep more time for eating and
  relaxation.
- I feel ashamed when I think of the things that I used
  to buy for myself earlier. I will definitely be more
  careful when shopping now. This period of fasting
  was a valuable experience.
- Fasting is now a part of me. Ever since the fasting period, the entire family has become a lot more
  conscious about their eating habits, the atmosphere
  at the table is a lot calmer, and fasting and eating have
  become an important topic of discussion in the family.
- I try to have a sort of a "remembrance day" once a
  week: a fruit-only, rice, or tea day.
- I became aware of my natural needs; for instance, I
  learned to relish the actual food and not just the coffee after that.

So what is preferable, fasting in everyday life or fasting in seclusion? Everything has a time and we should not compare these two types of fasting. Fasting in everyday life is the only possibility for many people because of time, family, or financial reasons. Even this type of fasting cannot be successful without proper motivation and a minimum level of calmness and time for self-reflection. This is because, as we have said repeatedly, fasting is not an automatic process. Whether it is done within the protected walls of a clinic, in a spiritual center, or under normal daily conditions, it is up to us what we make of it and how we create our fast.

© pzAxe - Fotolia.com

9

Mealtime

When we fast, break that fast, and then prudently rebuild our nutrition, we become aware of when we are satisfied and our body has taken in enough food. It teaches us to enjoy and appreciate the smallest of things all over again. After a week of fasting, baked potatoes with a little cottage cheese may be as good as a feast for you. When we leave out fattening extras, a potato starts tasting like a potato again and an apple taste like an apple. Fasting, then, doesn't oppose eating. On the contrary, through fasting we learn to improve our food and to enjoy it more. However, the reverse true, too: only a person who does not despise eating can come to love fasting. Therefore it makes sense for this book to include a reflection on eating.

Eating habits and lifestyle go hand in hand. This is not surprising since food, just like fasting, is a part of a complex whole and cannot be limited to just a biological function of ingestion. It is a part of the body and the soul and acts as a link between them. Eating and drinking make the body and the soul one unit. Food has great importance, not only for an individual but also for a community. Important events are celebrated by eating with friends and relatives. A favorite drink like wine is as much a part of such celebrations as flowers, singing, and music.

Food is considered to be a gift and every religion believes in starting and ending a meal with a prayer.

© Lisa F. Young - Fotolia.com

For instance, the following verses are recited in Zen temples before eating: "We are thankful to be having this meal. Because it is a fruit of other people's hard work and a result of the suffering endured by other forms of life."

Our eating culture is at risk, and this is not just a recent development. For instance, a contemporary of the emperor Napoleon reported that his manner of eating was too quick and improper, since due to his nature, he wanted everything at the same time. His domestic help was taught to serve him chicken, chops, and coffee all at once—anytime, anywhere. Today we no longer require domestic help; all we require is a little money to buy anything that is edible and available on almost every street at any time of the day or night: hot dogs, hamburgers, pizza, doughnuts, and so forth. Such "erratic eating habits" have completely taken over the lifestyles of people. For example, fast-food lovers have a particular kind of behavior that is not very different from Napoleon's: they often want to do two things at the same time and are eating only to get something into their stomach.

Fasting helps one realize how closely his or her eating habits and lifestyle are connected and how true the old saying is *We are what we eat.* And often we do not eat well. The problem is not just obesity or lack of healthy nourishment, but the carelessness of eating. Then what can one do? What should be our focus after a successful fasting period? Should we focus on our lifestyle or watch our eating habits? Since both of these are interlinked, there is no either-or. Both need to be checked and changed if required.

Lifestyle

Our world has become busy. There is too much to do and too little time, and somehow, we like it this way because it gives us a reason to run away from and avoid our own selves. This running away can surface in several forms: showing off and fussing around, workaholism camouflaging as hard work, consuming spiritual practices, and addiction in different forms.

But all these ways and means of escape cannot suppress our desire for peace and a different lifestyle. Quite a few people at some point during midlife begin to seek silence and to practice meditation. This inevitably leads to a new relationship with food as well. It is no coincidence that, for example, Zen cuisine does not use fish, meat, eggs, milk, or other dairy products and emphasizes eating only about two-thirds of one's usual quantity on days of intense practice. Apparently in this case, the practice of meditation has shaped the menu. And this is unsurprising, given that most spiritual practices also include rules for eating that are not fanatical. However one thinks about whole food diets and vegetarianism, it is undeniable that we are *what* we eat, and this will become even more important in the future.

Eating Style

How can we change our eating habits? The French epicure Jean Anthelme Brillat-Savarin answers this question in his standard work *The Physiology of Taste*, published in 1825 in Paris. His opinion on the prerequisites of an ideal meal is remarkably progressive. He says an ideal meal requires reasonably well-prepared food, good wine, kind guests, and—time.

Indeed, food, and especially the more elegant word *meal*, has a lot to do with time. "Mealtime" does not mean, as I once read in a fasting guide, that we are supposed to "mill" our food and that takes time. Although chewing is in fact important, the word *meal* originally meant a point in time. Because the time when all household members met for a meal was once the most important event of the day, this point in time, this mealtime, took on the meaning of eating. "Meal" is thus the "food served at a specified time." It has to be eaten regularly and on time and not according to one's whims and fancies.

And what is the logic behind phrases such as "Enjoy your meal" or "Blessing on the meal" that we use to wish others good appetite? First, we can understand this wish as the desire to take out time for eating, and for chewing, given that digestion starts in the mouth: well chewed is half digested! Second, this wish expresses the hope that mealtime be a time when we can be rejuvenated and refreshed in body and soul.

As Brillat-Savarin put it, "Indeed, after a good meal body and soul experience a great sense of well-being. Our facial expressions become more cheerful, meanwhile our spirit gathers new energy, our complexion becomes brighter, the eyes shine, and a pleasant warmth spreads throughout the body."[1]

Now you may ask, what does all this have to do with fasting? A lot! Fasting helps to develop healthy human eating and drinking habits and to keep in order or restore to order the desire for food, which is our most primary and fundamental drive. Fasting also helps us again to enjoy our food and our life. Onward then: Blessings on your meal!

Appendix 1

Misconceptions about Fasting

Fasting is basically about an all-encompassing motivation. I cannot stress this enough; it was the reason I wrote this book. And I wanted to present fasting in its three dimensions: the health aspect, the spiritual aspect, and the sociopolitical aspect. When writing about any one of these dimensions, my main concern was to ensure that the other two are also taken into account, and not to lose sight of the concept of fasting as a whole. I am now left with the task of clearing up three major misconceptions about fasting that I mentioned in the introduction. I am doing this with the belief that a revival of fasting can only happen once these misconceptions are cleared up and the extremism that jeopardizes fasting is avoided.

1. Diets Make You Fat

Today, nutrition has become a global problem. On the one side we have "too much" and on the other "too little," so that today we are threatened not only by hunger but also by unhealthy and excess nutrition. In his book *Weight Made Light*, Walther Zimmerman dares the thought that, just like the plague during the Middle Ages, obesity, until recently considered just a cosmetic issue, now has become an almost unsolvable problem.

Fasting offers a seemingly direct measure to fight obesity. The shortest way from excess to average, it is said, is shortage, which is called fasting. However, this can only work when a person fasts voluntarily and wisely and desires to change their daily habits. In addition to physiological concerns, psychological, spiritual, and social aspects always need to be taken into account with fasting. If this is not the case, then fasting is merely a slimming diet. More often than not, such slimming diets do exactly the opposite of what you want: they make you fat. And why is that?

It has been demonstrated that, besides lack of exercise and unhealthy nutrition, stress is a major cause of obesity. The following example may explain this:

> Mr. B is a bit chunky but not fat. He is transferred to another department where he has more work and a tense work environment. Mr. B puts on weight on the buttocks and stomach. In addition to problems with gas and slow bowels he also binges on bread and sweets. Reduced food

intake does not work for him, and on a slimming diet he loses weight everywhere except the stomach.

Mr. B is one of uncounted victims of a disorder of the pancreas due to constant stress over a long period of time. This results in indigestion and a steady overproduction of insulin. It is the job of insulin to transport blood sugar into the fat cells, and so more fat is created and lower blood sugar leads to spells of dizziness. It is therefore normal behavior to eat sweets, which are easily absorbable carbohydrates. However, this causes the body to produce more insulin, and the cycle continues. The increasing weight is itself a new stress factor leading to the obsession to lose weight. This is especially the case with women since being fat is not considered to be much of a problem when it comes to men.

This obsession with weight makes any diet a stressful event and leads to compulsive eating habits. Eating then can become a euphoric experience while at the same time being considered one's worst enemy—that is, the enemy of being slim. The body resists even the little food that it is given and digests it poorly, like an oven that is covered in soot or has insufficient ventilation and thus does not burn adequately. When we fast without proper motivation we will not be careful with breaking the fast and rebuilding our diet, which will not help our metabolism.

So how does one break out of this vicious circle? It is often enough to gain better insight into the context of nutrition and digestion. The saying, "If you are fat, you eat too much," is not always right. In his book *Fat and Skinny*, Jacques Moron differentiates between the "eat-obese" who take in a lot of food, and the "burn-obese" who eat normal or even low quantities of food but burn fewer calories for a variety of reasons, including too much stress, change in lifestyle, stress at work, or even the stress caused by the pursuit of thinness.

Knowing these things can have a very liberating effect. Cravings disappear, and the joy of eating can be restored, and often the joy of life as well. Diet addicts may also be helped by guided fasting, which takes into consideration the complexity of fasting and eating. They need not wage war against the desire to eat as if there is nothing good about it.

There is a very fine line between a slimming diet and a fasting course. I know people for whom a fourteen-day vacation that started as a slimming diet turned into an experience of authentic fasting and a time of regeneration and reorientation.

As we have already seen, correct fasting manages to do what slimming diets never or seldom can. It starts from complete motivation, subtly reorganizes the eating pattern of the body as "internal nutrition," frees the body from obesity as well as illnesses and pains, and protects it against any other ailments.

2. Hunger Strikes Need to Be Questioned

When people start a hunger strike, they are likely to put their health at stake for a crisis that cannot be resolved in any other way, or at least so it seems. It is not up to me to judge this form of radical protest. But I do believe that even a politically oriented fast needs to be subject to rules and guidance in the art of fasting. If this is not the case, a "hunger strike" can be over really fast, as in Otto Buchinger's example about five hundred workers in Silesia who went on a hunger strike. These five hundred protesters were waiting for their abstinence to bear results, and so it did: after just three days of not eating they were so exhausted that they could not even stand up on their own legs. This was hunger, not fasting!

How differently did Mahatma Gandhi approach fasting! For him, fasting was a subtle instrument that he never used as he fancied or because others insisted, but always at the behest of his inner voice. For him, the spiritual aspect was just as important as the political one and he always adhered to a set of rules that he himself had laid down. These included, among others, not thinking about food, drinking water, freshening up with a sponge, and sleeping in fresh air. As we all know, Gandhi's practice has become a model of politically oriented fasting.

3. Mandatory Fasting Had to Die

In the preface of Claude Régamy's book *The Rediscovery of Fasting*, Otto Buchinger shared his opinion that instead of being the very custodian of authentic fasting, the church, similar to the biblical parable of the talents (Matthew 25:24–30), has buried it in its fields and forgotten all about it. How could that happen over the centuries?

The causes for the decline of fasting lie as far back in time as Emperor Constantine and the formation of the Holy Roman Empire. Having become the state religion, Christianity submitted to the temptation to regulate religious life for everybody with defined rules and regulations. Regarding mandatory fasting, it was not the gospel's spirit of freedom that inspired it but the works of the early Christian apologist Tertullian (160–230 CE). In his work *On Fasting*, Tertullian opposes what he sees as the lax fasting practices of the Christians of his time and advocates fasting with such rigid determination that one might say that the better he demanded became the enemy of the good.

Officially the church rejected Tertullian's text on fasting but wasn't able to stand up to its challenge. Instead, the church submitted to its rigor and stayed infected with a false dualistic scheme that is foreign to the heart of the Christian message. This did not benefit fasting. When fasting is understood as the fight of the mind against the body, then, indeed, it will be directed against what is inherently good and life-giving in nutrition and the drive to eat. Such fasting becomes basically resistance; it does nothing to curb it, but rather suppresses our natural drive to eat and other basic drives. The unfailing disorder of these drives is not disciplined but, on the contrary, is bolstered. It is a simple psychological law: the more a drive is fought and suppressed, the more powerful it becomes.

Traditional religious fasting has ceased to exist with time, not because it was not spiritual enough but because it was understood far too unworldly. This is because, just as fasting cannot be understood as a purely biological phenomenon, we are also not allowed to disregard this aspect of fasting. We need the concrete experience of our own bodies in order to revive spiritually motivated fasting. In reality, compulsory fasting suffers from the same disease as any slimming diet because both try to separate what belongs together: body, soul, and mind.

Regarding uniform rules and regulations for fasting, neither individuals nor the community as a whole must unanimously be forced into fasting. The result would be what already happened: universal mandatory fasting failed to gain wide acceptance in spite of all the oaths, demands, and punishments. It is said that Charlemagne punished those who did not fast by sentencing them to death. While mandatory fasting was kept up, creative ways of circumventing it flourished. For instance, cooking seafood on days when eating meat was prohibited became popular, at least for those who could afford it. The purpose of fasting to give something up for the sake of the poor was converted into its direct opposite. One way of eating well was replaced on mandatory fasting days with another way of eating well. A long list of demands for fasting days was met with a cunning system that had the sole purpose of not having to comply with these rules. This hypocrisy was finally exposed. Books on morality that attempted to save mandatory fasting did not succeed; on the contrary, these proved to be the deathblow.

Mandatory fasting with its rules, prohibitions, and appeals, on the one hand, and an ingenious system of exemptions and immunities, on the other, no longer exists (and, I might add, "Thank God it doesn't!"). A wholesome practice like fasting challenges the whole person. It cannot flourish under force and joylessness. It needs the spirit of freedom.

Fasting is dead—long live fasting! Today the Lenten fasting period has taken on a new meaning for the church; one can find an increasing number of small, ecumenical groups who fast voluntarily for shorter or longer periods of time and thus experience how it positively affects mind, body, and soul; enhances the spiritual experience; and helps to open up to other people as well as to face environmental and global problems.

Appendix 2

Useful Tips

Note: The following are only suggestions to stimulate your thinking. This book is not intended to be a handbook for self-directed fasting. For that type of concrete treatment of fasting, see *The New Life Fasting Book*, advertised in the back of this book.

1. Fasting Drinks and Postfasting Diet

The following fasting menu offers a brief overview of a typical fast based on the Buchinger method:

- Mornings: 1 cup (8 oz.) tea with lemon juice
- At noon: 1 cup (8 oz.) vegetable broth (no vegetables), saltless
- Afternoon: 1 cup (8 oz.) tea with lemon
- Evening: 1 cup (8 oz.) fruit or vegetable juice

In addition, at least 35 to 50 ounces (1 to 1.5 qts.) of water during the day; this is a total of 210 to 260 calories.

Vegetable stock, fruit juices, and a spoon of honey (Buchinger method) make fasting easier psychologically and help in developing new eating habits. But they are not necessary. On the other hand, for older people, the drinks can include a glass of buttermilk (high protein content) in the morning and evening.

2. Postfasting

Breaking the fast: At noon one apple or a bowl of stewed fruit, chewed properly. Another apple or stewed fruit at about 3 p.m. For dinner a soup made from vegetables, or potatoes, rice, or oatmeal spiced with herbs and without salt.

The Buildup: 1st Day of Recovery (700 calories)

- Breakfast: Herbal tea, one apple, two slices of toast, cottage cheese
- At noon: Fresh salad, raw carrots or celery, mashed potatoes or rice, yogurt
- Afternoon: Tea with lemon
- Evening: Two apples, butter, cottage cheese, one slice toast, and tea

2nd Day of Recovery (1,000 calories)

- Breakfast: One apple, butter, two slices of toast, one glass buttermilk
- At noon: Fresh salad, spinach with mashed potatoes; yogurt as dessert
- Afternoon: Tea
- Evening: Fruits, one slice of whole wheat bread, butter, two tomatoes, a radish, and buttermilk

3rd Day of Recovery (1,100 calories)

- Breakfast: Muesli or granola, one teaspoon butter, one slice brown bread, one orange, and tea
- At noon: A plate of raw fruits, baked potatoes with herbed cottage cheese or Greek yogurt
- Afternoon: One glass buttermilk
- Evening: Fruits, rice or porridge oats, yogurt, one slice toast, one tablespoon cottage cheese, tea

4th Day of Recovery (1,200 calories)

- Breakfast: A bit of granola, two slices toast, one teaspoon butter, yogurt, or buttermilk
- At noon: Raw fruits, vegetables and Greek yogurt as side dish; fruits as dessert
- Afternoon: Fruits
- Evening: Mixed salad, brown bread, cottage cheese spread, herbal tea

5th Day of Recovery (1,500 calories)

- Breakfast: Muesli, two slices toast, one to two teaspoons butter, tea
- At noon: A plate of raw fruits, omelet with chanterelles mushrooms, Greek yogurt as dessert
- Afternoon: Fruits
- Evening: Two teaspoons butter, three tablespoons cream cheese, radish, baked potatoes, and tea

Continue with light vegetarian food for the next eight days before making a transition to a diet higher in protein.

Notes

Chapter 1

1. Von Seeland, "Über die Nachwirkung der Nahrungsentziehung auf die Ernährung." *Biol. Centralbl.* 7 (1887).
2. Guelpa, Guillaume. *La méthode Guelpa: désintoxication de l'organisme: Applications de cette méthode dans l'alcoolisme et les empoisonnements.* Paris: O. Doin, 1913.
3. Heinz Fahrner, *Fasten als Therapie: Physiologie und Pathophysiologie, Methodik, Indikationen und Verläufe, psychologische Aspekte* (Stuttgart: Hippokrates, 1985), 59.
4. Otto Buchinger, *Das Heilfasten* (Stuttgart: Hippokrates, 1979), 168.

Chapter 2

1. Anselm Gruen, *Fasten, Beten mit Leib und Seele.* Münsterschwarzacher Kleinschriften herausgegeben von Mönchen

der Abtei Münsterschwarzach, Bd. 23 (Münsterschwarzach: Vier-Turme-Verlag, 1984), 24.

2. Pie-Raymond Régamey, *Wiederentdeckung des Fastens* (Wien and München: Verlag Herald, 1968), 263.

3. Isaak von Ninive, as quoted by Régamey, *Wiederentdeckung des Fastens*, 95.

4. Heinz Fahrner, *Fasten als Therapie: Physiologie und Pathophysiologie, Methodik, Indikationen und Verläufe, psychologische Aspekte* (Stuttgart: Hippokrates, 1985), 49.

5. Régamey, *Wiederentdeckung des Fastens*, 49.

6. Basil the Great, "Sermon on Fasting," in *Texte der Kirchenväter. Eine Auswahl nach Themen geordnet*, Bd. 3, 285, ed. Alfons Heilmann and Heinrich Kraft (München: Kösel Verlag, 1964).

7. See also Otto Buchinger in Otto Buchinger, Jr., *Geistige Vertiefung und religioese Verwirklichung durch fasten und meditative Abgeschiedenheit* (Bietigheim: Lorber und Turm Verlag, 1967), 7.

8. Otto Buchinger in Otto Buchinger, Jr., *Geistige Vertiefung*, 11.

Chapter 3

1. Aristides, *Apology*, II c., http://www.earlychristians.org/how _did_they_live_1.html (accessed February 18, 2010).

2. R. Hugh Connolly, *Didascalia Apostolorum* (Oxford: Clarendon Press, 1929), 161. http://www.bombaxo.com/didascalia .html (accessed February 18, 2010).

3. Lanza del Vasto, cited by Pie-Raymond Régamey, *Wiederentdeckung des Fastens* (Wien and München: Verlag Herald, 1968), 40–41.

4. See the chapter "Saint Nicholas von Flue and Dorothea Wissling," in Ferdinand Holböck, *Married Saints and Blesseds: Through the Centuries* (San Francisco: St. Ignatius Press, 2002), 287–95.

5. Mahatma Gandhi, *Selected Political Writings*, ed. Denis Dalton (Indianapolis: Hackett Publishing, 1996), 87. http://books.google.com/books?id=Er59fRsspgoC&pg=PA87&lpg=PA87&dq=gandhi+nonviolent+fasting+role&source=bl&ots=dXJl2TTEia&sig=Qffnxi4UeU9TurlI9YQ23ocAH_I&hl=en&ei=lmF9S5zWK4Li8Qam-5zrBQ&sa=X&oi=book_result&ct=result&resnum=9&ved=0CBoQ6AEwCDgK#v=onepage&q=&f=false (accessed February 18, 2010).

6. Basil the Great, "Second Sermon on Fasting," http://bible.org/seriespage/appendix-1-basil%E2%80%99s-sermons-about-fasting (accessed February 18, 2010).

7. Mahatma Gandhi, *The Essential Gandhi: An Anthology of His Writings on His Life, Work, and Ideas*, ed. Louis Fischer (New York: Vintage, 2002), 182. http://books.google.com/books?id=gz6l-vCVgxQC&pg=PA182&lpg=PA182&dq=distress+remove+fast+and+pray+Gandhi+September+18,+1924&source=bl&ots=Ez2YnuezG2&sig=DqfMXoXOocs_WY2Zc58clGwz0L4&hl=en&ei=Emt9S-aTIpPf8Qa6tvHABQ&sa=X&oi=book_result&ct=result&resnum=2&ved=0CAkQ6AEwAQ#v=onepage&q=distress%20remove%20fast%20and%20pray%20Gandhi%20September%2018%2C%201924&f=false (accessed February 18, 2010).

Chapter 4

1. Pie-Raymond Régamey, *Wiederentdeckung des Fastens*, 258.

Chapter 5

1. R. Benz, ed., *Die Legenda Aurea*, 10th ed. (Heidelberg: J. C. B. Mohr, 1984), 184.

2. See Ruediger Dahlke, *Bewußt Fasten* (Münschen: Goldmann, 1980), 17.

Chapter 7

1. Otto Buchinger, *Das Heilfasten* (Stuttgart: Hippokrates, 1979), 65.
2. Niklaus Brnatschen, *Weg der Stille: Orientierung in einer lärmigen Welt* (Freiburg: Herder, 2004).
3. Max Picard, *The World of Silence* (Chicago: Regnery, 1952), 11.
4. Buchinger, *Das Heilfasten*, 65.
5. Picard, *World of Silence*, 11.

Chapter 9

1. Jean Anthelme Brillat-Savarin, *The Physiology of Taste* (New York: Penguin, 1992).

COMING IN AUGUST 2010
SELF-DIRECTED FASTING MADE EASY

THE NEW LIFE FASTING BOOK

SEVEN DAYS TO A SLIMMER, YOUNGER, HAPPIER YOU

Hellmut Luetzner, MD (Author)

Written by one of Europe's most experienced and renowned fasting doctors, this step-by-step reference provides daily guidance to complete a seven-day fast. The guidebook addresses a myriad of topics associated with fasting, including its history, common and successful forms, losing weight, overcoming temptations, and recipes for reintroducing food into the body. Additional topics relating to health and safety—such as keeping hydrated, staying warm, promoting circulation, and optimal body preparation for a fast—are discussed at length.

HELLMUT LUETZNER, MD, is a doctor who specializes in internal medicine with a focus on fasting. In 1975, he developed the fasting clinic in Germany, which he still heads today. He is the author of Successful Fasting: The Easy Way to Cleanse Your Body of Its Poisons.

Health, Nutrition
125 pages, Trade Paper, 6.25 x 8.5
25 Color Photos, 4 Charts, 4 Tables
Distribution Rights: US & CA

$16.95 (CAN $18.95)
9780824525903 (0824525906)
The Crossroad Publishing Company
www.crossroadpublishing.com